MANY STRUGGLES

West Indian Workers and Service Personnel in Britain (1939-45)

by Marika Sherwood

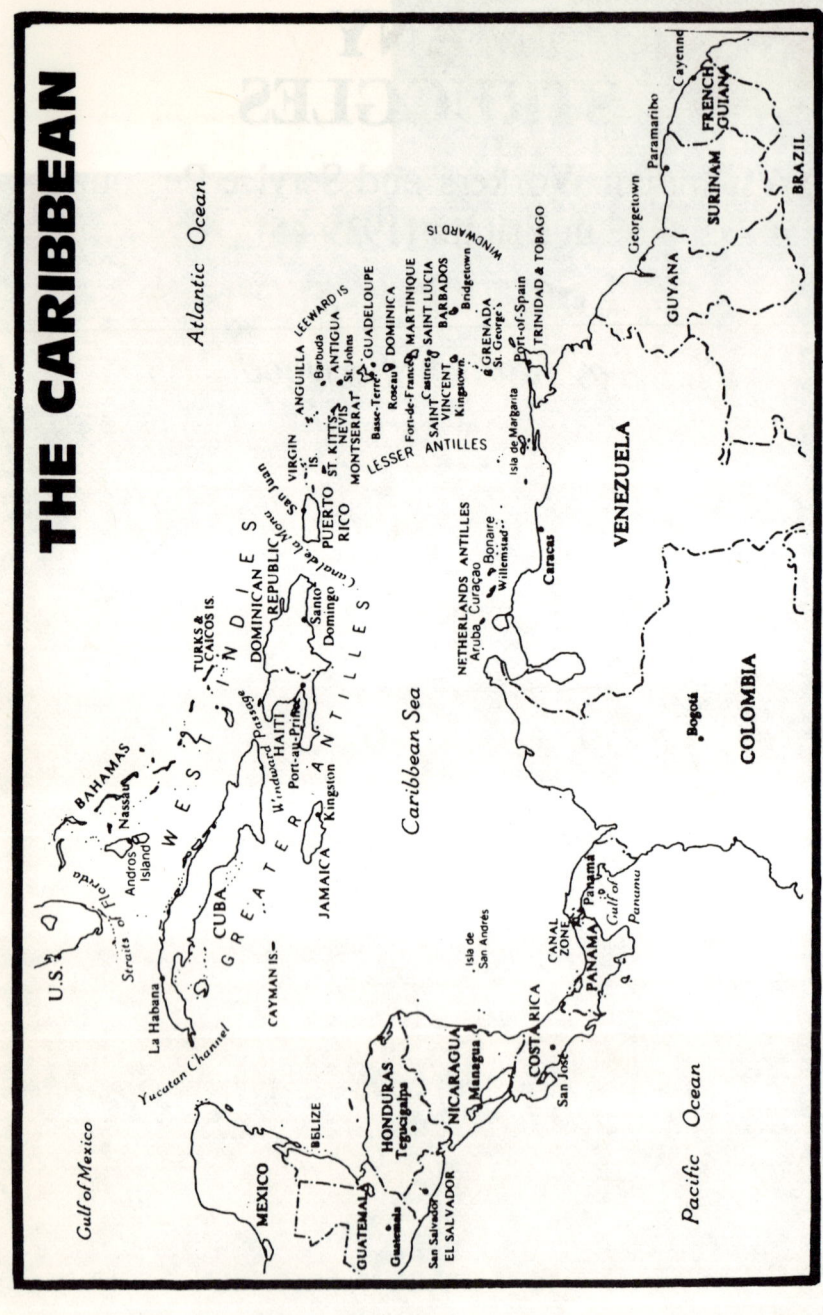

MANY STRUGGLES
West Indian Workers and Service Personnel in Britain (1939-45)

by Marika Sherwood

Karia Press

Many Struggles: West-Indian Workers
and Service Personnel in Britain, 1939-45.

First Published by **Karia Press** in 1985.

Copyright ©Marika Sherwood, 1984.

Typeset in Century by Bread 'n Roses.
Layout by Hilary Arnott
Cover designed by Buzz Johnson.
Military Photographs courtesy General Alfrey.
Printed by Whitstable Litho Ltd., Kent.

ISBN 0 946918 00 7 Pbk
ISBN 0 946918 04 X Hbk

Distributed by **Karia Press**
BCM Karia Press
London W.C.1N 3XX

CONTENTS

Acknowledgements
Abbreviations Used in the text
Publisher's Note

1. The Colour Bar in the British Military Services 1939-45	1
Introduction	1
PART I Removal of the Colour Bar?	3
1939	3
1940	6
1941	9
1942	11
1943	14
1944	15
1945	17
1946	20
1947	23
PART II HMG and West Indies	26
1939	26
1940	27
1941	30
1942	33
1943	34
1944	38
1945	38
1982	40
Footnotes and References	41
2. West Indian Munitions Workers in Britain	47
Introduction	49
The decision to Import West Indian Workers	53
Recruitment	58
Reception and Orientation	62
Housing	63
Employment	66
Employment: disputes	68
Employment: disputes re Promotion	69
Employment: Praise and Complaints	71

Unions	73
Welfare	74
Welfare: Sick pay	75
Wages and remittances	76
Unemployment	78
White attitudes & Practices toward West Indian Workers	79
The End of the Scheme	82
Repatriation	86
Notes and References	91

3. The British Honduran Forestry Unit in Scotland 93
    Introduction 95

British Honduras [Belize] 96
    Background information 96
    History 97
    Population 98
    Social and Economic Conditions 98

Recruitment 99
    British Honduras 99
    Britain 100
    Scotland 101

Arrival 103
    The First

Arrival 103
    The First Contingent 103
    The Second Contingent 104

Life in the Camps 104
    Clothing 105
    Food 105
    Medical Care 105
    Health 105
    Welfare 107
    Administration 108
    Conditions in the Camps 109
    Work 110

Relations with the local Community 112
    S.W. Scotland 112
    S.E. Camps 115
    The Northern Camps 118

Repatriation 118

The Men who Remained 121

The Men who Returned	122
Conclusions	124
Notes	127
References	130

4. West Indian Seamen: A Note   133

Footnotes and References   138

ACKNOWLEDGEMENTS

My Everlasting thanks are due to all those who answered my endless questions but especially to Richard Hart and Colin Prescod; whose patience with my naivety reflect their deep generosity; to Buzz Johnson who, through Karia Press, has arranged the publishing of the unsophisticated work of a near-sighted researcher, and to Craig, who has borne the vicissitudes of being my son with love and affection.

Sherwood, New York, March 1984

PUBLISHER'S NOTE

The contents of this book need no extensive introduction. The publication is an attempt, for the first time, to present some facts about the racism meted out to Black people by the British state during the Second World War. Many people do not know of the great problems the men and women from the Caribbean and other colonial countries, faced during the War at the hands of the British government and its bureaucrats and field officials. This is an attempt to present information which has been hidden from us. It does not pretend to be either a thorough analysis or a definitive piece of work.

The distorting of history and the spreading of lies and distortions are used to suppress peoples. Such techniques of psychological disorientation have always been used against those who strive for liberty and justice. So, the attempts to expose the racism experienced by those who came to Britain to serve in the cause of Freedom between 1939 and 1945 is also an exercise in combatting the efforts to suppress us.

We also know that the policies meted out to those Blacks did not develop there and then. Furthermore, those practices intensified in Britain itself after the Great War. What we understand is that the practics of racism has a long history; it has continuity. It is flexible and comes in different clothes — different costumes — at different times in history and varies to suit different conditions.

The treatment of Black people in Britain during the War was, therefore, an extension of the historical racism and oppression imposed on them by the European colonial and Imperial powers.

The essays contained here seek to contribute to arriving at an understanding of the true experiences of, and state responses to, the first large contingents of Caribbeans to labour in Britain itself. These served in various sectors and contributed towards the fight against Fascism. We have dealt with four areas. They relate to the racism in the British military services, the experiences and institutional responses to munitions workers, the Forestry workers who came to Scotland to work in the Timber industry, and a shorter introductory note to the West-Indian seamen.

References to official files and documents are given to ease the work of the others who will undoubtedly continue in the development of research in the area. We especially look forward to seeing Black people respond for they are the ones who will take up the mantle and challenge the positions taken by the backward elements in the field. We also hope that the work which is to come will be 'written' by the real makers of history to bring forward the actual positions and experiences of the people who actually experienced the experiences we wish to inform about.

SOME ABBREVIATIONS USED IN THE TEXT

NAACP	National Association for the Advancement of Coloured People
ECAC	Executive Committee of the Army Council
RAF	Royal Air Force
CO	Colonial Office
FO	Foreign Office
ROF	Royal Ordnance Factories
YMCA	Young Men's Christian Association
LCP	League of Coloured Peoples
GTC	Government Training Centre
ILO	International Labour Office
OTC	Officers' Training Corps
ARP	Air Raid Precaution Service
ATS	Auxiliary Territorial Service
NCO	Non-Commissioned Officer
WRAC	Women's Royal Auxiliary Corps
NAAFI	Navy, Army & Air Force Institute

Colonial resources are

THE way to bring the war to a successful end is so to organise your resources and to bring such pressure on the enemy as to stop him from having the ability or heart to continue the fight. Trinidad has kept that principle in mind and has co-operated with great efficiency in the great task of beating the Axis.

PETROLEUM

Trinidad has endured the hardships and inconveniences that are inseparable from a global war because she realises that small variety of diet and poor transport are but petty hardships compared to the mighty effort necessary to win victory.

In common with other West Indian Colonies, Trinidad has made a very great contribution to the war effort by co-operating in the lease of naval and air bases to the United States of America.

The arrival on the shores of Trinidad of survivors from torpedoed merchant ships and the news of U-boat sinkings in the Caribbean Sea have proved that the war is still uncomfortably close to Trinidad and the people are answering the call to maintain and increase the strength of their own Civil Defence organisation. Local Civil Defence is desperately important in a war such as this when the actual battle area can change almost overnight.

Many men from Trinidad are on active service in Britain with all three Services. A Royal Naval Volunteer Reserve was established in 1940 in Trinidad and five times the number of men needed immediately applied for enlistment.

Women of Trinidad have volunteered for war work overseas and some are

PITCH LAKE

serving with the A.T.S. and W.A.A.F. in Great Britain. Many others have joined the Red Cross or other nursing services. In Trinidad itself women have taken part in the " Win the War Association," a voluntary body which organises such things as local food production and the collection of salvage.

VITAL TO THE WAR EFFORT

FISHING

Trinidad knows of the importance of freeing shipping for carrying troops and ammunition to distant battlefronts—without adequate shipping the victory of Tunisia could not have been won—and is answering the call to release more shipping by developing local food cultivation and local fishing. Rice is now being grown in Trinidad for home consumption and new factories have been opened to turn local raw materials into products for home consumption. These include factories for the manufacture of margarine, matches, condensed milk and biscuits.

Trinidad has natural resources which are of vital importance in time of war. These are petroleum and asphalt. Petroleum in particular is drastically important in a mechanised war, so Trinidad has concentrated on raising her output which is now considerably above the 1938 level.

Many contributions towards the prosecution of the war have been made by Trinidad. Up to March 31st, 1943, the people of Trinidad had contributed over 800,000 dollars to the Bomber Fund. This fund has already supplied three bombers and twenty fighters to the Air Ministry. The "Win the War Association" had collected over 292,000 dollars in voluntary gifts by the same date.

MARGARINE FACTORY

The local branch of the British Red Cross Society had been given over half a million dollars by the end of March, of which 40,000 dollars had been subscribed during the first three months of the year. The War Savings movement had yielded 1,177,000 dollars in War Savings Certificates sold at the General Post Office by March 31st, 1943.

NATIONAL SAVINGS

JAMAICA
for Victory

MONTEGO BAY

1. The Colour Bar in the British Military Services 1939-45

INTRODUCTION

The Manual of Military Law, in a paragraph headed Limited Power to Enlist Aliens, states that the *"number of aliens in any corps is not to exceed the proportion of 1 to every 50 natural-born subjects"*. Then, inexplicably, unless the Army looked upon all Blacks as aliens, the paragraph continues: *"A relaxation in favour of negroes and persons of colour was originally made in consequence of negroes captured in slavers being taken into the service of the Crown, and was continued to legalise the recruiting of natives on the West Coast of Africa for service in the West India Regiments (now disbanded) and of Lascars in the East; and the relaxation has been extended to inhabitants of British protectorates in order to enable troops raised in the East and West African protectorates to serve outside their boundaries"* (p. 217). Thus Section 95(2) of the Army Act permitted the enlistment of *"any negro or person of colour"*. However, in 1938 an amendment was passed (Army Order 89 of 1938) by the Army Council, restricting entry to men of pure European descent. The amendment was made *"to regularise a semi-official ruling because of the difficulty in placing a coloured British subject who had enlisted in this country in 1936. Until the amendment was made, the only way of excluding undesirable non-Europeans was by telling the Examining Medical Officer to find them unfit or by some other equally undesirable subterfuge"*.[1] Obviously, by this reasoning, all non-Europeans were undesirable, and rather than have to resort to subterfuge, which, after all, was ungentlemanly, it was much preferable to institutionalise the colour-bar. The Military Colleges, where officers were trained, had, in any case, only accepted men of pure European descent who were the British-born sons of British-born parents.

The Navy and the Air Force were equally racist. Section 95 of the Air Force Act stated that enlistment was only open to men of pure European descent, though aliens could be accepted; officers had to be not only of pure European descent, but British subjects as well. The Navy's officers were also limited to British subjects of pure European descent. Ratings could be *"Maltese and Men of Colour who are the sons of British-born subjects . . . Men,*

1

however, who are themselves British subjects may be entered as Officers' Stewards and Cooks under non-continuous service engagements on the Africa, East Indies and China stations, irrespective of their parents' nationality . . . Men of colour, even if British subjects, have no claim to count their time towards pension unless they entered the Service before 1st January, 1904" (Para. 385 of Navy Regulations). As *"British-born"* meant born in Britain, the Navy was hardly likely to be troubled by vast numbers wanting to enlist; and, as if it were not enough to accept British-born Blacks for service jobs only, as far away from Britain as possible and without pension rights, para. 386 of the Regulations restricted the numbers of *"Maltese and men of colour entered for non-continuous service as an Officer's Steward or Cook"* by requiring *"special and prior Admiralty sanction"*. Furthermore, the interpretation of these Regulations regarding the entry of ratings, as explained by the Secretary of the Principal Personnel Officers Committee at a meeting on 27/4/45, in fact constituted a colour bar. The entry of Maltese or men of colour as ratings was not excluded, the Secretary said, *"but the entry of these for other than local service was subject to special Admiralty sanction. In practice, the cases that came up were usually those of half-breeds and the decision depended mainly on the 'Britishness' of the man's appearance and habits"*.[2]

In Part I this paper will detail the discussions within the government regarding the removal of the colour bar. In Part II I shall examine how the new rules affected the use of West Indians during the war. Unfortunately so many of the government files have been destroyed that many discussions trail off virtually in mid-sentence: for instance, in the CO968 series, of the ten West Indian files listed in the Register of Correspondence, only one remains. I have been unable to extract any pertinent information from any branches or associations of the Army, the Navy or the Air Force.

PART I
REMOVAL OF THE COLOUR BAR?

1939

By the end of 1939, after exerting continuous pressure on the armed service chiefs, the Colonial Office succeeded in getting their agreement to the raising of the colour bar. Why did the Colonial Office, normally racialist in its attitude towards Blacks, go to so much trouble? Did it undergo a sudden change of heart? This was clearly not the case as the Colonial Office colluded with the other government departments in ensuring that, as far as possible, the lifting of the colour bar should only be a public relations exercise. But the question still remains: why go to so much trouble? The answer undoubtedly lies in the dual functions the Colonial Office had to perform: controlling the Empire and ensuring that while Britain was fighting a war against racist Germany, Britain should not herself be accused of racist practice. Thus, being charged with the oversight and surveillance of Black colonials in Britain, the Colonial Office had to be seen to bow to pressure being brought by these colonials against the colour bar. Also being charged with the control of the colonies, and bearing in mind the recent uprisings in the Caribbean, the Colonial Office could not take the risk of agitation throughout the Empire against a codified colour-bar. It would have been politically and practically inexpedient to have to send troops to control rebellious British subjects in the colonies while Britain herself was engaged in a supposedly anti-racist war in Europe. A public relations exercise would serve to quieten the colonials and forestall criticism from either Britain's foes or allies.

Members of the approximately 15,000 strong Black community in Britain began complaining about the colour bar in the armed forces early in 1939. In April, Black students from Cambridge, Oxford and Newcastle Universities and from Aggrey House (a residential hostel in London for African students), who had tried to enlist or enrol in the Officers Training Corps (OTC) complained that they had been barred on racial grounds. On May 2nd the Colonial Office held a meeting to discuss the problem. Those at the meeting *"appreciated that the employment of large batches of coloured men would give rise to difficulties"*, but as they had learned that at least one Black man in Cardiff had been allowed to join the Air Raid Precaution Service, they decided to make a 'semi-official' approach on the matter to the War Office.

The approach elicited a reply from the War Office dated 26/7/39, which stated that the *"Army Council was considering this thorny problem"*. To the Army Council, General Finlayson had recommended that (1) commissions should be reserved for British subjects of British parents of pure European descent; (2) as the Royal Navy and the Royal Air Force did not need extra men, there was no need to change the rules barring men not of Pure European descent; (3) Blacks resident in Britain should be registered but not called up for training once conscription was introduced. General Finlayson's rationale for retaining the status quo, i.e., barring men not of pure European descent from the armed forces, was that the main role of the army overseas was *"policing duties"* and Blacks obviously could not be used in this role. He also maintained that Blacks could not be kept *"in the UK permanently"*.

Thus did General Finlayson articulate the fear of Blacks becoming resident in Britain; a fear which had been present in the relations between the English and Blacks since the sixteenth century, when Elizabeth I demanded the deportation of Blacks resident in London.

While negotiations were proceeding between the Colonial Office and the service chiefs, **Dr Leo March**, a Jamaican born dental surgeon, wrote to the Colonial Office on 26/9/39 that he had applied to join the Royal Air Force and had been turned down on the basis that he was not of pure European descent. In internal memoranda Colonial Office staff discussed Dr March and the case of Arundel Moody, son of Dr Harold Moody, the President of the League of Coloured Peoples. Arundel, an ex-public school boy, with 6 years in his school's Officers' Training Corps, had been refused by the Tank Corps because he was not of pure European descent. Mr Lees noted that there would shortly be an announcement lifting the colour bar; *"this does not, of course, mean that British subjects who are obviously men of colour will in practice receive commissions"*, only that such men will not be turned down on the basis of not being of pure European descent at the recruiting offices. He advised that Dr March should not be encouraged to reapply *"since for the obvious reasons I feel that his* *chances of getting a commission would be rather small".* Mr Calder concurred that it would be *"unlikely that the RAF will give a commission to a black dental surgeon".*[3]

It was probably by agreeing to collude with the de facto policy of retaining the colour bar that the Colonial Office managed to convince the recalcitrant service chiefs to accept a change in the publicly stated policy. Whether these negotiations were conducted by telephone, or by correspondence now destroyed, we do not know. One letter only remains, from Winston Churchill, then First Lord of the Admiralty, to Malcolm MacDonald, Secretary of State for the Colonies. Churchill wrote consenting *"to your request that British subjects of non-European descent should not be barred from service in the Navy or the grant of commissions by reason of their racial origin".*[4] On October 19, simultaneous announcements were made in the House of Commons by MacDonald and in the House of Lords by the Secretary of State for India, the Marquess of Zetland: "... **During the present emergency,** *Indians, Anglo-Indians, Burmans, British subjects from the Colonies and British protected persons who are in this country, including those who are not of pure European descent, are to be on the same footing as British subjects of pure European descent as regards voluntary enlistment in the armed forces and as regards eligibility to be considered for the grant of emergency Commissions in those forces. This principle will apply in the case of all three Services."* (Emphasis mine.)

There is considerable evidence that the announcements were not meant to affect actual practice. The Foreign Office advised its Consular Offices on November 10 that *"only offers of service from white British subjects should be considered".* The Colonial Office sent telegrams marked 'Secret' to all Colonial Governors advising them that *"it is not desirable that non-European British subjects should come here for enlistment".*[5] On January 6, 1940 the Colonial Office informed the Cabinet that what must evidently have been their decision had been put into effect: *"Colonial Governments have already been informed that it is not desired that non-European British subjects should come here for enlistment".*[6]

At the recruiting stations Blacks were being told that they were ineligible for enlistment as if the October announcement had not been made. The League of Coloured Peoples wrote to Mr. MacDonald on 8/11/39, complaining about the delay in the granting of commissions to colonials resident in Britain. They cited the cases of Dr March, still refused by the Royal Air Force; Dr Otto Wallen of Trinidad, refused by the Royal Army Medical Corps; B. O. Alikaja from British West Africa, A. K. Petersen from Southern Rhodesia, and S. Kennard to British Guiana, who held a pilot's licence, all turned down by the Royal Air Force. Though not on the League of Coloured Peoples' list preserved in the archives, Ghana-born Dr Wellesley-Cole was also excluded by the services. In an article in the March 22, 1982 issue of *West Africa*, Dr Wellesley-Cole wrote that at the outbreak of the war he was a *"self-employed doctor in England . . . I applied to join the armed services"*, but together with other Black doctors was turned down as *"we were not British Subjects of Pure European Descent"*.[7]

Mr MacDonald's staff informed him, while a reply was being considered, that the *"final decision in individual cases for emergency commissions must lie with the Service authority. Actually special pressure has been brought on the War Office to give preference in two cases — Dr March and Arundel Moody, despite the fact that direct entry to the Officers Training Unit has been closed since October 21, 1939."* MacDonald duly replied to Dr Moody on December 4, that his son and Dr March had been accepted; however, *"henceforward, except in the case of certain specialist categories (such as doctors), entry to the Officers Training Unit will only be open to men who have first served a period in the ranks"*.[8] As far as I have been able to ascertain Arundel Moody was the only Black Briton to receive a commission in the British Army during the entire war.

1940

In January the Colonial Office received a letter of complaint from a Mr K. A. Ward, a Barbadian student studying medicine at Edinburgh. Mr Ward, who had previously worked as a motor engineer, tried to enlist as a flight mechanic. He had been told that only men of pure European descent were acceptable. The Colonial Office advised him to reapply. On reapplying, Mr Ward was told that he was unskilled as he had only had 2 years experience as an engineer, and that only men of pure European descent were being accepted as unskilled recruits by the Royal Air Force. This forced the Colonial Office into having to complain to the Air Ministry, who replied that the Royal Air Force had no use for unskilled men and the *"information regarding regulations for unskilled men not of pure European descent was unauthorised and contrary to instructions"*.[9] One can only presume that instructions to exclude Blacks on some grounds other than that of not being of pure European descent either had not reached or were ignored by this particular recruiting officer.

Dr Moody had not been deluded by the Secretary of State's letter of December 1939. He became involved, as the April 1940 *Newsletter* reported, in the cases of George Price and R. Spiers. George Price had tried to enlist in the Royal Air Force but was not accepted by the recruiting officer because he was 'coloured'. He turned to his clergyman, the Rev. C. A. Smith for help. Mr Smith journeyed to Glasgow to make representations on Price's behalf; he was told that only men of pure European descent could be accepted. Price's brother then enquired at the Royal Navy recruiting office on George's behalf: he too was told that only men of pure European descent were acceptable. Price's case was taken up by *The Scotsman* and then by his MP, Mr Woodburn. On January 24, 1940, Mr Woodburn asked in Parliament, why George, whose British West Indian father had served in the British Navy during World War I, had been rejected because of his colour by both the Navy and the Air Force. Captain Hudson, Civil Lord of the Admiralty, replied that *"George C. Price had never applied to join the Royal Navy"*. This, of course, was true: he had been told not to bother applying as he would not be accepted! Mr Woodburn was as persistent in his questioning as Captain Hudson was in his reply that George Price *"has not applied"*. The matter rested there.[10]

The *Newsletter* in April carried the text of Mr MacDonald's reply to Dr Moody's letter of complaint regarding Price. *". . . The standard nationality rule for entry into the Royal Navy is that candidates must be British-born sons of British-born parents . . . I am sure that any man of colour who, fulfilling the above condition, now presents himself for enlistment, will not be turned away on the ground of colour . . . "* (Price's father was born in Jamaica; his mother was of Danish origins; George was born in Edinburgh.) This reply highlights the speciousness of the October announcements: by not lifting the requirement that recruits must be British-born subjects of British-born parents, the Royal Navy, the Royal Air Force and the **army officer** corps hoped to avoid having to accept any Blacks as they obviously presumed that there would be *no* Black British subjects with British-born parents. Whether the parliamentarians knew that this ruling existed but accepted the armed services' sophistry, is a moot point.

The Colonial Office was, however, sufficiently distressed by all this publicity regarding Price and subsequently Mr R. Spiers' similar experience, to question the Royal Navy and the Royal Air Force. In the ensuing correspondence the Admiralty was adamant that Blacks were not wanted in the Royal Navy. As Winston Churchill was still First Lord of the Admiralty during the exchange of letters, he must be held culpable of the perpetuation of the colour bar in the Navy and the speciousness of the public announcement of October 19th. As must the Secretary of State for the Colonies, Malcolm MacDonald, who advised his staff that though *"they* (the Admiralty) *are contravening the October decision, if all publicity can be avoided, that might be all right. But can we avoid it?"*

Accordingly, another letter was sent to Mr Farrell at the Admiralty: *". . . Mr MacDonald presumes it will not be necessary to make public that such relaxations of the standard nationality rule will as administrative acts be made only in the cases of candidates of pure European descent. He fears that any public announcement on such lines would be challenged as a breach of the Government undertaking of October 18 and that great harm might be done in the Colonial Empire by the apparent breach of faith. Is it possible to ensure that any Admiralty announcement regarding relaxation of the standard nationality rule refers only to specially recommended candidates whose parents were naturalised before the birth of the child?"*[11]

As no further correspondence with the Admiralty has been preserved and none remains of that with the Royal Air Force, we can only presume from material in the *Newsletter* that the Royal Air Force and the Royal Navy won the day and that further adverse publicity was avoided. The August 10 issue of the *Newsletter* printed the Air Ministry's June 6 reply to Dr Moody's remonstrations regarding the continuing exclusion of Black candidates: *". . . for the period of the war, British subjects from the Colonies who are in this country, including those not wholly of European descent, are to be on the same footing as British subjects from the United Kingdom as regards eligibility for voluntary enlistment in the Armed Forces, including the RAF*

"...". However, it was not until the end of the year that the first men not of pure European descent were enrolled in the Royal Air Force. The December *Newsletter* reported that George Price had been accepted by the army and that the first African had been selected for pilot training by the Royal Air Force.

The Royal Navy continued its racist practices. On August 21 the Second Sea Lord approved recommendations for new Nationality Rules Regarding Entry, thereby institutionalising the Navy's colour bar. The new rules stated that though at the outbreak of war the requirement that recruits should be British-born sons of British-born parents on both sides was modified to *"British-born sons of naturalised parents, provided both parents were naturalised at the time of the candidate's birth"*, the *"exception now proposed to the standard rule should not apply to men of colour. The practical rule for them to remain at present, i.e., (they must) satisfy the standard nationality rule."* The instructions issued to the Recruiting Staff Officers on August 28 stated, inter alia, that *"Coloured men are not accepted to serve for long term engagements"*. Under Section B recruiting officers were instructed that *"Candidates to serve for the period until the end of the present emergency should also normally be British born and the sons of British born parents; for this type of engagement however British subjects from the Colonies and British Protected Persons who are in this country (i.e., Indians or Colonial Natives) are eligible to be accepted provided they are British born and the sons of British born parents. Such applicants should be considered on their merits with other candidates. Whilst coloured men are not theoretically excluded from the exceptions, in practice* **no coloured man who is not British born and the son of British born parents would be regarded as suitable for acceptance.**" (Emphasis mine.)[12]

1941

In the words of Dr Wellesley-Cole, *"the realities of the 1939-45 war soon forced the acceptance of black Britons into the forces as officers, starting with the Royal Air Force, from Sierra Leone, Nigeria and the Caribbean"*. The acceptance certainly had to be forced and referred to acceptance only for the duration of the war. Neither was the acceptance wholehearted. The League of Coloured Peoples' *Newsletter* for August 1945, carried the statement of an Indian airman that he had experienced the colour bar in canteens, hospitals, dining halls and sleeping quarters. His was not an isolated experience as similar complaints occur throughout the government files.

During the war, permanent commissions could only be granted to Cadets under training in Cadet colleges or to members of the universities' Officers' Training Corps. There was therefore a problem with Black students applying to join the Officers' Training Corps. The Colonial Office won a partial concession from the War Office on this point in December 1940: applications from Black colonial students wishing to join their university's Officers' Training Corps would be referred to the Colonial Office for approval which the Colonial Office would only grant if there was *"a reasonable probability that the applicant would be accepted as a commissioned officer* **in the local forces of his Colony**". (Emphasis mine.)[13] The Colonial Office based its recommendations on information solicited from the Colonial Governors regarding each student who applied. W. L. M. Garcia, whose Jamaican-born parents were British nationals, was accepted by the Colonial Office for the Leeds University Officers' Training Corps in March 1941; T. H. Clerk from Ghana was accepted but S. Ntem refused also in March; A. J. Williams from Nigeria was accepted by the Colonial Office in June 1941. It is curious to note that of these 4 men, 3 have European names; one is therefore left to wonder whether one parent of each might not have been European and thus whether the new criteria for admission might not have been a 'shade' and not a colour difference.

The Colonial Office also raised the question of enlistment in the **regular** army. Paragraph 2(c) of the Army Council Instruction 101 of 1941, which was an unaltered updating of previous ACIs, stated that *"only British subjects of unmixed European descent will be accepted on a normal Regular Army engagement"*. The War Office informed the Colonial Office on 12/7/41 that this policy would not be reversed, because *"a large part of the Army served abroad and it would be undesirable to have coloured men in the ranks of British units in India, Egypt, Singapore, etc."*. The new Secretary of State for the Colonies, Lord Moyne, asked the War Office *"not to prejudice further discussion on this"*. But the War Office's final word on this issue, on December 2, was that Blacks *"would not be taken on Regular Army engagements because then the peace-time Army would contain the very* *elements which we think it ought not to contain"*.[14]

Having lost that struggle, the Colonial Office took up some of the most blatant contraventions of the 1939 announcements. When it was learned that paragraph 35(b)(v) of the War Regulations for the Voluntary Aid Detachments stated that SRNs had to be *"British subjects, daughters of British subjects and of pure European descent"*, the War Office was asked for clarification. The Matron-in-Chief agreed to remove the clause on November 10. Whether the Air Raid Precaution Service, which came under the aegis of the Home Secretary, or the Auxiliary Territorial Service, and the Voluntary Aid Detachment, both under the War Office, ever wholly removed the colour bar is not known. On November 8, 1941 an advertisement appeared in *The Scotsman "Women between the ages of 18 and 40 are invited to enlist for general service overseas in the ATS. They must be British subjects of pure European descent"*. There is no record of the Colonial Office objecting to this. A few Black women and men were accepted by the ARP, the ambulance service and in the mobile canteens and First Aid units, though at least in the ARP the common excuse of *"fellow workers would object to the presence of coloured people"* was used to exclude Blacks from some stations. At least one Black woman was excluded from the Women's Land Army by her local country because of the *"difficulty of finding a billet for her"*.[15]

1942

From this year onwards there is a great paucity of relevant files at the Public Record Office; for 1942 all that remains is some information regarding the situation of Black British subjects and Afro-Americans in the US who wanted to help Britain.

Towards the end of 1941 an Afro-American pilot, Mr C. M. Ashe, applied to join the RAF Ferry Command. When he was told that only members of the *"white race"* were acceptable, Mr Ashe complained to the NAACP, who passed on his complaints to the British Embassy in Washington. Simultaneously the NAACP complained about the Red Cross, which was then recruiting doctors on behalf of the UK government and had rejected Dr King, an Afro-American, on the basis that *"only white citizens of the US are eligible"* The Embassy forwarded these complaints to the Foreign Office in London. Though the Air Ministry had told the

Foreign Office on 22/1/42 that "*'white race'... has now been withdrawn by the Ferry Command*", the Foreign Office asked the Embassy to only "*inform the NAACP if you are pressed...For your information, our reply will in the main provide reassuring answers to the Association's complaints*". On March 27th the NAACP was eventually informed that "*This condition is not in accordance wih the views of HM Government and Mr Churchill is informed that it has been deleted and that each case will be considered on its merits.*" As the allegations regarding Dr King were highly embarrassing and the government was seriously concerned about its image in America it was decided to circulate the proposed reply to the NAACP to all the Ministries concerned for their approval before sending it on to the Embassy. The text which was eventually approved and forwarded to the US in February read: "*British children who do not know the traditional kindness shown by coloured people to children, might be uneasy through unfamiliarity... The coloured population of the British Isles is not as large in proportion as that of the US ... some people might even never have seen those of a different colour. In adopting the policy which led to the refusal of Dr King's offer of service, there was no reflection, therefore, implied on the professional competence of those whose generous offer was not accepted*". Whether the NAACP found the British Government's dissembling 'reassuring', neither the British government nor the NAACP files reveal.[16]

Regarding British Blacks in the US, or elsewhere, who might want to enlist in the British forces, the Foreign Office advised all consuls of the decision made by the Overseas Manpower Committee on Volunteers from Abroad. The circular, marked 'Confidential', in Paragraph 8 on 'Colour' noted that "*generally speaking there are few opportunities at present for the employment of volunteers of the coloured race in the UK. These should not, therefore, be accepted without reference to the Foreign Office ... it is of the greatest importance to avoid any suggestion, verbal or by procedure, that there is any discrimination of this kind in the treatment of the volunteer. If other grounds for rejection do not exist, names should be referred to the Foreign Office.*"[17]

On July 30, the Embassy in Washington, bearing in mind the concern of the NAACP and the situation within the US, wrote to the Foreign Office: "*The coloured question is tending to become more acute in this country at the moment and it is important that we should not give any grounds for suspicion that we are deliberately discriminating against coloured volunteers . . . if, therefore, any appreciable number of coloured British subjects respond to the coming appeal and volunteer for service in the UK, I may find it necessary to urge that special arrangements be made to accept a reasonable number . . . even though their actual value in the UK may not be very great."* Why the value of *"coloured volunteers"* may not be very great, the Embassy did not discuss. The Foreign Office replied on August 12 that it *"is important that coloured volunteers should not actually be accepted without reference to me. Indiscriminate acceptance of any large number for service in the UK would create a most difficult situation with which we are not prepared to deal . . . Hitherto we have found it impossible to accept independent coloured volunteers, but we have recruited complete units from the West Indies with some success. Experience shows however that it is essential that such units should be fairly rigidly segregated . . . We hope to make arrangements on these lines for any coloured British subjects who may volunteer in the US . . ."* A telegram three days later clarified that the *"segregated units may have been for civilian work . . . not recruited by the War Office".*[18] One might, of course, wish to question the whole notion of 'success' when it is coupled with segregation.

However, the shortage of skilled men had obviously become so great in Britain that by August 18 the Foreign Office informed the Embassy that the army had decided to accept *"coloured tradesmen"*: a further telegram dated August 29 stated that the RAF would also accept skilled men but *"the Admiralty prefer not (repeat not) to consider any coloured British subjects".* Another telegram on September 29 reiterated that it was *"essential to avoid all (repeat all) unskilled British subjects".* The Embassy reported on November 1 that they tried *"to find some technical grounds* (for rejecting unskilled Black British subjects) *and do not of course indicate that our refusal is due to the fact that the men are coloured".* On November 29 the Embassy emphasised that *"we cannot guarantee that there may not be trouble in rejecting coloured British subjects wishing to transfer to British forces from US forces. If you confirm that no such optants can be accepted for the British forces it might be possible for us to arrange for their acceptance by the Canadian army in which coloured units exist".*[19]

While the Foreign Office was thus implementing the Cabinet's decisions regarding British Blacks, the War Office informed the Foreign Office that the Commander-in-Chief in the Middle East had turned down the idea of using Afro-American labour units as they would have to be paid more than local labour. Did the Foreign Office think that it would be possible to raise labour units in 'American countries' with low pay rates? Mr Evans of the Foreign Office commented in an internal memorandum dated May 19: *"utilisation of the considerable pool of negro labour from the West Indies would be the best solution . . . evidently the War Office want their niggers cheap"*. Unfortunately the files do not reveal how or why the War Office ever considered using Afro-Americans, or why it ranked these men higher in its racial hierarchy than the West Indians whom it had persistently refused to use (see Part 2). The Foreign Office dealt with the War Office's political naivety succinctly, writing on June 6 that there were *"insuperable political and practical objections"* to the proposal.[20]

1943

Towards the end of 1942 it was announced that *"the sole criterion and qualification for selection for the regular army will be fitness in every respect to hold a regimental commission"*. Furthermore, *"officers from the Colonial Forces, who have undertaken a liability for General Service"* would also be acceptable. The Colonial Office was pleased with this announcement but queried the War Office as to whether the new regulations included coloured Colonial officers. (There were by now a few Black officers on Governor's Commissions in the Colonial forces.) The War Office's reply to persistent questioning throughout the whole year was that *"the matter is still under consideration"*.[21]

Why the War Office decided not to inform the Colonial Office that a decision had in fact been taken, must have been a matter of strategy on how to handle what the War Office must have seen as an importunate Ministry. The decision which had been taken at the Executive Committee of the Army Council (ECAC) meeting on August 6 stated that *"candidates (for the regular army) must be British subjects, sons of British subjects and of pure European descent"*.[22]

We have one piece of evidence that the non-acceptance of Blacks as army officers, even as doctors, continued throughout the war. The August 1943 issue of the *Newsletter* reported that though Dr Moody had been assured on November 16, 1941 by the Director General of the Army Medical Services that the Service would accept Blacks, Dr Moody had discovered that the June 1943 regulations for the Service still contained a clause restricting entry to men of pure European descent.

1944

On February 29 the British Consul in Atlanta, USA, wrote to the Washington Embassy that he had been accepting a few volunteers, but *"in accordance with your instructions, we do not accept coloured volunteers"*. He also advised that the Jamaican Government had informed him that it was difficult to continue rejecting Blacks' passport/visa applications; in order to avoid an *"unfortunate incident"* could the UK issue instructions that only applications from British-born West Indians should be accepted? The Foreign Office duly passed on this request to the Colonial Office, who instructed their British West Indian Governors accordingly.[23]

This further demonstrates the iniquity of the British government and its Foreign and Colonial Office officials. It also highlights how the law of racial equality, promulgated on October 19, 1939, was consistently and persistently contravened by various administrative measures. In the words of a Colonial Office officials, *"we must keep up the fiction of there being no colour bar"*. Both the government tactic and the *"fiction"* are alive and well in 1983.

During this year the debate within the army and the Air Force regarding the admission of Blacks into the post-war armed forces, whether as other ranks (ORs) or as officers, continued. As the Royal Navy had remained adamant in its exclusion of Blacks during the war, the question, in their minds, certainly did not arise for the post-war era. However, as increasing numbers of Blacks were serving in the army and especially the Air Force where many were distinguishing themselves as officers, the question had to be addressed.[24]

The Air Council discussed the issue at a meeting on October 3. The Chief of Air Staff wanted to retain the pure European descent clause; the Vice Chief mentioned the difficulty of posting coloured men; the Air Member for Training also advocated the retention of the pure European descent clause on the basis that

15

the "*susceptibilities of the Dominions*" had to be kept in mind. However, the Secretary of Air argued against the retention or the reimposition of the colour bar on the grounds that it would be "*indefensible and barbaric against an officer who had earned the DFC... I am not disposed to agree to a colour bar*", Sir Archibald Sinclair said, and announced that he would explore the issue with the other services.[25]

At its meeting on December 1, the Executive Committee of the Army Council received a Paper on Nationality and Descent by the Colonial Office, which outlined the current position: Colonel Stanley "*felt very strongly*" about the colour bar in commissions in the regular army; 'coloured' men had held King's (or Governor's) Commissions during the war; the numbers of officers "*would not in any case be very great . . . the outlet in the colonies is insufficient for an able and energetic officer because the forces there are too small . . .*"[26]

The Principal Personnel Officers of all the services had discussed the Paper and reported to the Executive Committee of the Army Council that they "*were inclined to favour the retention of the colour bar*", though they "*appreciated the political difficulties*". They stressed that all three services "*must keep in step on this issue*". One reason they gave for retaining the colour bar was that those men already in the services who wanted to enlist or transfer to the regular army had been asked to register; as pure European descent had not been published as a condition of eligibility, Blacks who had registered would have to be "*weeded out when the final reports are checked*".[27]

The members of the Executive Committee of the Army Council discussed all these recommendations. The Adjutant General was in favour of retaining the colour bar. The rest agreed: "*it is clear that the general feeling of the committee was strongly in favour of the retention of the pre-war rule of pure European descent. It was clear that the admission of non-Europeans into such units of the British Army would not only have many embarrassing repercussions, but might well have adverse effects on the discipline of British white other ranks . . . The difficulty did not lie so much in the exercise of powers of command over white troops by coloured officers . . . the present war to some extent familiarised white troops with this necessity in various theatres. The difficulty lay more in the constant association of white and coloured officers in normal day-to-day peace-time routine of regimental life, and it* was unlikely that such associations would be successful in practice."[28] However, it was decided to form a committee to consider both enlistment and commissioning in the peace-time army.

On December 4, the War Office informed the Colonial Office that the colour bar would be retained because *"British troops do not take kindly to being commanded by coloured officers ... Further, the presence of coloured officers in a unit in peacetime is apt to be a source of embarrassment"*.[29] Colonel Stanley replied on December 22 that he could not accept the colour bar; the Government's position was against it; he would take the matter up with the Cabinet.

1945

Within a couple of months and perhaps because elections were imminent, Stanley changed his mind about approaching the Cabinet. He wrote to his counterpart at the War Office on February 27: *"you will appreciate that I do not wish to trouble the War Cabinet myself with this at the present time ... I hope you will agree not to issue any regulations on this subject which contain a colour bar clause without first taking the matter to the War Cabinet"*.[30]

The committee which the Executive Committee of the Army Council had decided to set up in December 1944 was duly formed. The Chairman was Major-General J.F. Hare; the members were Brigadier E.J. Medley, Lieut. Col. W.E.G. Williams, Brigadier J.D. Woodall, and Mr Lambert. The Committee on Post War Regulations Respecting the Nationality and Descent of Candidates for Entry to the Army met four times and reported to the 207th meeting of the Executive Committee of the Army Council held on March 30.

The Report began by summarising the situation regarding recruits of non pure European descent: though there was no legal colour bar to commissioning or enlistment, the military colleges only accept men of pure European descent who are British subjects and the sons of British subjects; by Army Order 89 of 1938 enlistment in the ranks was restricted to men of pure European descent. Until this Order was made, *"the only way to exclude undesirable non-Europeans was by telling the Examining Medical Officer to find them unfit or by some equally undesirable subterfuge"*.[31]

The 'evidence' collected was also summarised: General

Sir Giffard had said that it might be *"possible to have African commissioned officers in an African Army ... He found the standard good between officers and men of the same race but he did not consider it possible to establish a satisfactory relationship between non-European officers and the British other ranks. The former would never be able to achieve proper appreciation of the social and domestic problems of the latter"*.[32] The Director of Biological Research in a written memorandum submitted that *"The objections, if any, to the employment of coloured men in the Army are due to social and economic considerations and are largely a matter of prejudice"*. The Director of Personnel said that *"During the present war difficulties have arisen from giving coloured other ranks powers of command over white troops ... he knew of no actual case of difficulty arising from a coloured officer exercising powers of command over white troops. He thought that such incidents had been avoided by careful sorting of units"*. The evidence of the Director of Staff Duties *"was to the effect that good non-European candidates for commissions have intellect, industry, conscientiousness and reliability. It is however, characteristic that they are loath to take the initiative or to exercise strict command. They show less practical sense of things and problems. Although of pleasant personality, invariably experience has been that this is of the negative sort and probably derives from an inferiority complex ... the reaction of white candidates to coloured candidates is on the whole good, but is inspired almost wholly by compassion ..."*[33] These comments by the Director can either be seen as pure racist cant or as a prime example of how little white officers understood Blacks — officers or other ranks. Or both.

Not surprisingly the Committee reached the following conclusions:

"(a) They consider that although non-Europeans may possess many of the necessary officer qualities, the crux of the matter is the question of racial and traditional background. It cannot be expected that such officers will be able to establish the relations with their men which are essential if leadership is to be fully exercised. They feel that man-management would never be satisfactory and in particular that the officer could never be capable of dealing with the family and domestic problems of his men. They are, therefore, unanimously opposed to the commissioning of men of non-European descent in UK forces.

(b) The Committee also feel that the enlistment of non-Europeans in UK regiments and corps of the Regular Army is undesirable. The case is perhaps not quite so strong as it is against commissioning, but there are two good reasons. Firstly, there is evidence that in general the non-European is not acceptable as a companion and brother-in-arms to the British soldier. Secondly, it is considered that in the post-war Army it will be essential that no man entering the ranks should be regarded as ineligible for a commission as would be the case if our views at (a) are accepted.

(c) If it is considered politically undesirable to maintain an express bar in the regulations:

> *(i) the Committee ... feel that it would be dishonest to remove the express bar from the regulations and leave the whole onus for non-selection on the selecting authority... There should be a clear statement of Government policy to the effect that only those persons should be granted commissions in UK regiments and corps who have a British social and traditional background and who prove by their service in the ranks and to the satisfaction of the selecting authority that they are capable of gaining the respect and appreciation of British other ranks and of leading them in battle, and that the non-European who is seeking an Army career should seek it with men of his own race, i.e. the Colonial Forces.*

> *(ii) as regards enlistment, as there is no machinery for selection, there is no alternative to retaining the bar in the regulations without placing an intolerable burden upon the recruiting authority."*

The Committee therefore recommend:

"(i) That, if politically possible, the existing ban on the commissioning of men not of pure European descent should not be removed, but if it must be removed it should be replaced by a very full statement of Government policy. This policy should be that except in very exceptional cases such men will not be commissioned into UK regiments and corps of the British Army but that they should be given an opportunity of serving as officers in the Colonial Forces in which they would only be required to command men of their own race.

(ii) That men not of pure European descent should not be allowed to enlist in UK regiments or corps of the Regular Army."[34]

The Executive Committee of the Army Council considered the Committee's Report, accepted the recommendations and asked the Chairman to submit this decision to the Secretary of State.

As no further Colonial Office records on this subject have been preserved, we do not know what the Colonial Office's reaction was to the ECAC decision. From the Air Council Minutes for the 11th meeting of 1945, we learn, however, that Secretary for the Colonies, having found it impossible to achieve consensus among the services, decided to approach them individually. He asked the RAF to relax its nationality rules as *"unobtrusively as possible"*.[35] On November 19, the Air Minister, Lord Stansgate, advised the new Secretary, George Hall, that *"the colour bar will not be introduced into any of our regulations for commissioned officers or other ranks"*. Hall, aware of the previous nefarious practices of the services, thanked Lord Stansgate in a letter dated December 11, in which he hoped that *"Everything possible, will, I am confident, be done to ensure that the importance of your generous policy is not hindered by officers of too rigid a mind who cannot believe that a coloured man could ever satisfy the exacting conditions for entry."*[36]

1946

Having succeeded with the RAF, George Hall continued the Colonial Office's struggle with the army and the navy. His letters unfortunately have not been preserved; two of the replies are, however, still in the files.

The First Lord of the Admiralty wrote to Hall that the RN's *"regulations have been in force for many years ... I cannot see my way to amending them. I recognise however that the question may have to be submitted to the Cabinet"*.

The new Minister for War, J.J. Lawson, also wanted to retain the colour bar in the army. In his letter to George Hall he repeated the old ECAC position and offered a new argument of his own: those Dominion Governments which maintained a colour bar amongst their own people would be embarrassed by Blacks in a British army whose major peace-time task was 'keeping order' in the Empire.[37]

Secretary Hall obviously meant business as he outmanoeuvred the Ministry for War. Mr Lawson was forced to report to the Army Council on April 12 that questions had been asked in the House of Commons on the colour bar in the army. Furthermore, *"The Colonial Secretary had agreed, on political and social grounds, to the abolition of the colour bar in the Colonies. It had further been agreed that Colonial troops should be officered by personnel of their own colour. He was being pressed to agree to the principle that there should be no bar against coloured officers serving in the British Army. Should the Army refuse to accept this principle, the Colonial Secretary would bring the matter before the Cabinet for decision. He had already received a copy of the draft paper prepared by the Secretary. He felt that, in practice, even if the principle was accepted, there would be little danger of any coloured personnel becoming officers. He therefore considered that, in view of the negligible risk, we should agree with the suggestion of the Colonial Secretary . . . The Air Ministry had agreed to the principle of coloured officers, provided that the applicant was a resident in this country at the time when application for a commission was made, and that he had the necessary qualifications."*[38]

During the discussion following the Minister's remarks, the old arguments and fears were repeated; if the colour bar were removed, the army would have to return to the old ploy of using administrative measures to keep Blacks out. The Deputy Chief of the Imperial General Staff, Sir Ronald Weeks emphasised that *"It was only natural that one country should not want to be led by the nationals of another country . . . (in any case) only white officers should lead British troops"*. Did Sir Ronald foresee not only the dissolution of the Empire but the coming of the Nationality Act of 1982 that he thus summarily declared Black colonials non-British? Or is it that the most fallacious of arguments can be used by the most eminent of men when advocating racist principles?

The Secretary of State closed the meeting by proposing that the Executive Committee of the Army Council should *"accept the principle on account of the very small risk involved. He realised, however, that the other Members of Council were unanimously opposed to this view, and he requested that a paper should be prepared for circulation to the Cabinet setting out their views. He would reserve his own opinion for oral presentation when the Cabinet met."*[39]

The Paper prepared for the Cabinet by the Permanent Under

Secretary reiterated all the previous arguments against the admission of Blacks into the army. The only new point raised was that as Blacks would form a small minority in any army unit, their life would probably not be very happy; and *"coloured families in married quarters would introduce a dangerous complication ... there would be a risk of incidents"*. Where the danger lay the Under Secretary did not specify. He did, however, confirm that with the exception of about 12 Medical Officers, all the Blacks commissioned during the war had received King's Commissions, which were for service with Colonial forces only.[40]

The First Lord of the Admiralty also had a Paper prepared for Cabinet discussion. The First Lord was *"opposed to altering the normal rules of the Royal Navy ... which in the event would be one of form only and not of real significance. Commonwealth interests would be injured more severely if some years after relaxing our regulations it was disclosed that no coloured officers, had, in fact, been entered."* Clearly, whether by overt regulations or covert administrative manipulations, the Royal Navy was determined to prevent Blacks enlisting.[41]

The Secretaries of State for India and the Colonies in their Paper argued that in any case there would be very few candidates; the Colonial forces were too small to provide an outlet for able men; Blacks born and brought up in the UK would again be excluded. They urged that *"the matter should be considered against the background of Imperial policy in the widest sense. The future of the country may well turn upon the success with which we can ensure the co-operation of hitherto dependent territories, as they achieve self-government, in upholding and presenting to the world British ideals and the British outlook upon social and political problems. The desire for such co-operation on their part cannot be encouraged by regulations which reflect the old attitude of racial superiority."*[42]

There is no record of the Cabinet having discussed these Papers. What we do have, however, is the brief by the Executive Committee of the Army Council for their Minister to prepare him to deal with the arguments they thought the Secretary of State for the Colonies would present at the Cabinet meeting. If Mr Hall questioned why *"if we enlist and commission coloured persons in time of war, why not in peace? The answer is that in war we were forced to use many expedients which are undesirable in peace."* Those Blacks born and bred or domiciled in Britain who wished to serve in the armed forces should be sent to *"serve with a native force"* in one of the colonies.

A new argument was propounded: *"There have been no means of judging the effect on American opinion of the commissioning of coloured persons, but it is thought that the feelings of those who come from the Southern States, at any rate, would be outraged. The effect on public opinion in South Africa, where racial prejudice is possibly more acute than in the USA, would be profound."* The brief concluded by advising that *"if the Cabinet decide against you, you should enter a warning that there are important financial implications which will demand further study."*[43] Presumably the 'financial implications' were that as Blacks in the British army would have to receive the same pay as whites, 'native' troops might then also ask for the same pay.

1947

While Tom Driberg, Major Wilkes and a few others continued raising the colour bar question in Parliament, in May the Secretaries of State for India and the Colonies approached the Cabinet again. Their Paper related that they had obtained a compromise from the army and the navy, whereby *"a more active and positive policy of giving men and officers from colonial local forces suitable facilities for training with the Royal Navy and the British Army"* would be pursued. However, they were not satisfied with this and wanted the colour bar removed. To the arguments presented in 1946 the Secretaries added two new points:

1) under the present system it was impossible to test out whether *"coloured entrants could be absorbed without friction: or if Black officers could successfully command white troops"*;

2) there was no opportunity for British Blacks resident in Britain *"who might well provide some of the best coloured candidates for the Forces"* to join the army or the navy.

The Secretaries stressed that the perpetuation of the colour bar was *"contrary to the declared policy of H.M. Government towards the peoples of India, Burma and the Colonial Empire ... It can hardly be argued seriously that the admission of a few non-Europeans into the Navy or the Army in any year can make an appreciable difference to the efficiency or wellbeing of these Forces; on the other hand, automatic exclusion on the ground of colour, even of a few candidates, may have serious political consequences."*[44]

The Paper presented by the First Lord of the Admiralty simply repeated all the reasons given in the previous year for barring Blacks from the Navy.[45]

Unfortunately the Paper by the Army has not been preserved. The 'secret' brief by the Executive Committee of the Army Council for their new Minister, Mr Bellenger, repeated the warning about financial implications. On the morning of the Cabinet meeting the Minister received yet another, hastily prepared brief. The ECAC, furious at the new National Service Bill, which did not exclude Blacks, reinforced their previous anti-Black position and warned that by administrative action they would *"refrain from calling up persons who are coloured."*[46]

The Cabinet met on June 3. The Secretary of State for India, embroiled in the struggle being waged for India's independence, warned that the exclusion of Blacks would be greatly resented in India. The Secretary of State for Air said that 'coloured men' were admitted into the RAF *"in recognition of the distinguished services which many such men performed during the war"*. The numbers, he noted, were not large. The First Lord of the Admiralty admitted that a few short-service commissions had been granted to non-Europeans during the war. However, in view of the fact that *"serious complaints already received from ships in which coloured men from India and Egypt were receiving short-service training"* and as *"the decision to admit coloured entrants would have an adverse effect on morale and discipline . . ."*, he was against the lifting of the colour bar. The Secretary of State for War warned that discipline would be undermined if men ever had to serve under Black officers; if coloured other ranks were admitted, they would have to be eligible for commissions, and *"the British soldier will not take kindly to serving under coloured officers"*. The spokesman for the newly created Ministry of Defence said that as no decision had yet been reached about the future size of local forces, it was *"premature to reach a decision about lifting the ban on the entry of non-Europeans in the Royal Navy or the Army"*.

Despite all these dire warnings, *"the general feeling of the Cabinet was that it was difficult to justify the retention of the*

ban. *Raising of the ban would not result in a flood of applicants
... possibility of trouble could be further reduced by careful
selection. There would be no need to give wide publicity to the
Government's decision."* It was therefore *"agreed that British
subjects of non-European descent should be admitted to the Royal
Navy and the British Army provided they attained the requisite
standard, were resident in this country, and could satisfy the
selection authorities that they were likely to mix with other entrants
and hold their own in the corporate life of the Services."*[47]

In 1948 the colour bar was finally removed from the army and navy recruiting instructions. How frequently the new administrative ploy clearly permitted by the Cabinet, that Blacks could be rejected on the assumption that they would not mix well with other recruits, was subsequently used, we do not know.

PART II
HMG AND WEST INDIANS

1939

Cabinet began discussing the use of colonial manpower in September 1939. The Secretary for the Colonies then reported that though there was a *"wave of intense loyalty"* in the West Indies, the Governor of Jamaica had cautioned that this *"may not be maintained unless suitable openings can be found for utilising the numerous offers of service for military and other duties"*; Sir Arthur also protested against the colour bar for commissions. The Governor of British Guiana had also warned that the lack of public works, lack of opportunity for enlistment and rising prices might lead to more labour troubles.[48] The most pressing problem, the Secretary said, related to the West Indies: it was essential to convince West Indians that *"their assistance is needed and valued ... It is a matter of first political important to effect this ... The War Office should agree to an early raising of military units there."* The First Lord of the Admiralty, Winston Churchill, suggested that African and West Indian troops should be used in various parts of the Empire in order to relieve the regulars for service in France. The Adjutant General said he would oppose commissions for Blacks in the UK though he was not against commissions in the local forces. He deplored that by the new National Service Act *"coloured British subjects would be admitted to the Army."* The Cabinet decided that the War Office and the Colonial Office should look into the best use of colonial and particularly West Indian manpower.[49]

At its meeting on September 28 the War Office decided that *"consideration will be given to the desire of the West Indies to form a combatant unit"*; it was thought that the islands would be a good source of labour units and that recruitment for such would be enhanced by the formation of a combatant unit. The possibility of *"altering the rules regarding commissions for West Indian gentlemen"* would be examined.[50]

On October 5 the Cabinet received among the various Departmental Reports one on the Colonial Empire: *"In certain colonies, especially in the West Indies, it will be of the first political importance to provide opportunities of service overseas in a combatant unit or units; it is accordingly hoped that it will be possible to authorise the Governors concerned to make an announcement in the near future to the effect that HMG are prepared in principle to agree to the raising of such units at a later date... It is hoped at a later stage to send more detailed advice on the long range question of the utilisation of manpower (especially European manpower)... West Indian Governors... being asked to advise as to the possibility of raising labour units for service with the General Duties Corps of the Army."*[51]

On October 9 the War Office issued recruiting instructions. Among these was the requirement that men from the colonies who volunteer should be sent to the Colonial Office for a letter of recommendation. On October 19 the colour bar in the armed forces was lifted. On October 27 the Colonial Office informed the West Indian Governors that both the Army and the Air Force needed skilled tradesmen; the RAF also needed qualified pilots and aircrews. But obviously the War Office had reached a decision at least about West Indians who might have thought of coming to the UK to enlist: the Colonial Office sent telegrams to the Governors saying that *"it is not desired that non-European British subjects should come here for enlistment. How you handle this we leave to your discretion."*[52]

1940

The detailed advice on the Utilisation of Manpower Resources of the Colonial Empire, marked 'Secret' was presented by the Secretary of State for the Colonies to the Cabinet in January 1940. The Colonial Office's opinion on West Indians was particularly low and contained serious disinformation. *"West Indian combatant units (of coloured men) would be of doubtful value for combatant service overseas, especially against German troops in Europe. Broadly speaking, it may be said that in the last war the battalions of the British West Indies Regiment were found to be more useful as pioneer units than as combatant troops... For political reasons, it may be necessary, in order to satisfy local amour-propre, to raise a small combatant unit in the West Indies for service there or overseas."*[53, 54] The notion that local troops should replace the

European garrisons on the islands was discussed and dismissed. It was thought that West Indians would be of most use as pioneer troops, but as the USA was enquiring about their use as labour on the Panama Canal, it was hoped that the problem might be solved by sending unemployed West Indians there.

Officially, of course, this could not be communicated to the Colonial Office. Thus the War Office wrote to the Colonial Office on 8/2/40, saying that because men from the tropics cannot stand the climate of Europe, the decision regarding the use of pioneer units from the colonies was being postponed. However, as the German advance swept all before it, and portions of British divisions had to be sent as labour corps to aid the British Expeditionary Force, in March the Colonial Office again raised the question of the use of West Indian labour at a Cabinet meeting. Mr MacDonald pointed out that France was planning to use labour corps recruited in Morocco, Algeria, Madagascar and Indo-China. The estimated numbers required would be 25-30,000 per month. In the light of this, would it not be possible to also use British colonial labour? The War Office promised to examine the question.
question.

The Colonial Secretary's concern was not with the question of the War Office's attitudes towards colonial labour. The Secretary's job was to keep order in the Empire, and there had been considerable disorder in the West Indies. From 1935 onwards, waves of strikes and rioting had spread through the islands: the people were protesting against their lack of rights as workers and voters; against un- and under-employment, low wages, lack of educational and medical facilities. At the beginning of 1940 the Under Secretary of State for the Colonies, Lord Dufferin, had received a letter signed by a number of companies in the islands regarding *"attacks on employees and other persons exercising authority"*. The companies wrote that *"a general impression, sedulously fostered by propagandists, that these outrages reflect only bad living and working conditions has been passively accepted, whereas we attribute them to formentors of trouble interested not in improving conditions but in sowing discontent"*. Major Orde Browne, Special Labour Advisor in the Colonial Office, was asked by the Under Secretary for his comments. The Major wrote, but not until some seven months later, that *"Disorders occur (when there is) unemployment, low wages, distrust, absence of regular means whereby feelings of the potential disorderlies may be made known to those in authority . . . Underemployment is the cause of well-founded discontent, but suits the employers . . . The attitude of the employers is as much in need of attention as that of the employees . . . their constant ineptitude and gaucheries . . . It is plain they are not putting their minds to labour problems as they do to others with which they are faced".*[55]

The Colonial Office also had to contend with pressure from the island Governors who felt that West Indians, as there was no longer a West India Regiment, should be accepted into the British armed forces. For instance, the Governor of Trinidad wrote on May 22, 1940, that Trinidad *"merchants are anxious to equip and send white men . . . they had sent 270 during World War I . . . It is necessary to afford an outlet for the strong local desire to render loyal service . . .".* The Colonial Office replied in dismay on May 25: *". . . is there any danger of similar arrangements for coloured men? . . . By the October announcement . . . it was never contemplated that coloured persons should be specially sent to England for enlistment".*[56] But the Trinidadians meant business: a public meeting was held in Woodford Square in Port-of-Spain at the beginning of July; a resolution was passed and forwarded to London. The Trinidadians asked Her Majesty's Government to use 25,000 men from Trinidad as part of 250,000 men of a West Indian Corps; they *"also feel that it would be most unfair to our Mother Country should we not like our English brothers also taste the horrors of actual warfare and the unspeakable sacrifices attendant thereto . . . We realise that we can be very useful service in the defence of our Home shores."*[57]

The West India Committee, a London-based group representing the plantation interests in the islands, also urged the Colonial Office to press for the acceptance of West Indians in the British Army. The Jamaican Banana Producers Steamship Company offered free passage to men accepted by the services. The Governor of Jamaica warned on May 29 that *"there is no doubt that recent events have accentuated in certain sections restiveness to feel they are doing something to help".*[58]

The Air Ministry, though it had not regarded Blacks as suitable for aircrew duties in 1939, reversed its decision in by the end of 1940. In a letter dated November 11, the Ministry informed the Colonial Office that it would accept radio mechanics, wireless operators and aircrew from the colonies, provided the *"coloured men were really skilled and considered by the local Selection*

Board to be suitable to associate with British airmen ... Special care should be exercised in their selection".[59]

1941

In January the Air Ministry extended its requirements to include fitters, metalworkers, electricians, instrument repairers and machine tool setters. By February the Ministry was so worried about aircrew numbers, that the West Indian Governors were cabled that the *"Ministry was anxious for a constant flow of aircrew recruits, European or non-European".* By April, however, the Ministry, on the basis that it was *"clear that non-Europeans require about half as long again to complete their training as the normal British entrant"* asked the Colonial Office *"to consider informing the Colonial Governors that the recruitment of non-Europeans should be slowed down".* Mr W.J. Bigg replied to Wing Commander J.A.C. Wright, stressing the political importance of continuing to recruit in the Caribbean as enlistment in the RAF was affording *"colonial personnel their only opportunity of combatant service";* and there were so few suitable candidates anyway![60] Given that in AIR 2/8355 the report on the first six men accepted for pilot training shows 82-90% for Ground Examinations, one 'average' and five 'above average' for Flying Assessment and comments that the men's *"mental alertness is above the average pupil",* it is very difficult to understand the Wing Commander's comments about training. Whether owing to the pressure from the Colonial Office, or because whatever the real objections had been to 'coloured' entrants had been removed, on May 24 the Ministry informed the Colonial Office that the position had been reconsidered: 421 recruits including 234 non-Europeans would be accepted up to March 1942; however, in future elementary mathematics would be required for all wireless operators and gunners. A few days later the Ministry informally discussed with the Colonial Office the possibility of recruiting men from the West Indies for ground crew duties.

It took the War Office until the end of the year to make the decision to enlist men not of pure European descent for the Army. It was agreed to accept skilled tradesmen, between the ages of 20 and 45, who had a *"reasonable standard of skill, were fit for general service in the Army";* family allowances would be payable;

acceptance to a particular trade depended on passing a test and enlistment was to be for the duration of the war. The Governors were informed of this decision on 17/1/41. Men had to be certified fit by each colony's Medical Officer and the colonial government had to test and certify each applicant's skill; those accepted had to sign an undertaking to enlist on arrival, though final acceptance depended on passing another medical examination in the UK; pay would begin from the day of attestation only, but the War Office kindly undertook to pay for the voyage and the cost of the medical examinations. The Governors were further advised that men over 45 or those under 45 who had not passed the colonial medical examination but who were skilled fitters, welders, blacksmiths, coppersmiths, sheet metal workers and machinists would be accepted for munitions work in England.[61]

The very limited number of men now eligible for overseas service, either as skilled tradesmen in the Army or as aircrew for the RAF, did not ease the Jamaican Governor's problems. On February 12 he cabled the Colonial Office: *"We feel that if Jamaica could send overseas one battalion the effect on local opinion would be excellent. By limiting the numbers to one battalion good men could be assured".*[62] Doubtless it was this, the resolution from Trinidad and probably similar pressure from the other islands' governors not preserved in the Public Records Office, which forced the Executive Committee of the Army Council to again consider the question of West Indian recruitment. The Executive Committee of the Army Council decided not to *"recruit coloured West Indians either as combatant troops or as labour units"*. The decision was based on the following considerations: (a) West Indians were undesirable in the light of the experience of the last war; (b) it would be difficult to employ West Indians as labour units in the UK because of the climate, difficulties with billeting and the difficulty of providing such a unit with British staff; (c) West Indians might be absorbed in employment on building the US bases in the Caribbean — *"indeed, there might be some objection on the part of the US to the competition which would be afforded in this respect by recruiting labour companies for the British Army"*. However, ECAC conceded that if it were *"necessary to recruit West Indians as a political gesture, there was a possibility of employment in the middle East"*. The Commander in Chief would have to be consulted; it would be difficult to arrange shipping.[63]

It seems that this decision was not communicated to the West Indian Governors, as on July 15 the Jamaican Government again cabled the Colonial Office: "... *physically fit young men, but not of RAF standard, anxious to go to the UK to join the fighting forces. May they go?*"

Mr Williams, chairman of the Jamaican Producers' Association, not having received a positive reply from the Colonial Office to the offer of free passages to Britain, began making approaches to the Canadian Army to see if West Indian volunteers would be more welcome there. The War Office was no more anxious for West Indians to serve in an Empire army than it was for them to serve with the British Army. In a letter to the Colonial Office dated 13/9/41, which clearly illustrates their scathing attitude towards West Indians, the War Office wrote: "... *the proposal will doubtless gratify the political aspirations of the people of the West Indies, namely to serve abroad in the fighting forces ... at the higher Canadian rates of pay ... May cut right across the interests of the schemes, now under consideration, to recruit dock and labour battalions in the West Indies for service in the Middle East.*" There is some evidence that the War Office communicated to Canada its desire to maintain a reserve army of labourers in the West Indies in case it ever found a use for them. Possibly due to such pressure, or due to their own racism, the Canadians refused to accept West Indians volunteers, as the Jamaican Governor informed the Colonial Office: "*Canada says it already has more volunteers for the Air Force than it can deal with and Jamaicans would not stand the Canadian climate if in the Army*".[64, 65] The excuse given by the Canadians, the climate, is clearly nonsense, as Canada had been importing West Indians since 1911 to work in her mines, shipyards, ships and railways.

By November, Lord Moyne, now Secretary of State for the Colonies, accepted that the War Office would never use West Indians as combatant troops; however, he continued to press for their employment in pioneer units. On December 7, Margesson, following Anthony Eden as Secretary for War, once again firmly rejected West Indians, citing shipping difficulties.

The Ministry of Labour, a little more realistic about manpower shortages (eg, it was estimated that the armed forces requirements for skilled engineers from 1/6/41 to 31/12/41 would be 25,835, but only 8,660 men would be available) proposed to the Lord President's Committee on 19/12/41 that free passage should be paid to men and women from the colonies who were prepared to join the armed forces or accept service as civilians. The Colonial Office thought that *"Labour's proposal probably relates to men of European descent only ... Our difficulty is that the War Office refused to have such (pioneer) units either in this country or any other war zone such as the Middle East"*.[66] Labour, however, did not mean European-descent only, and, despite some members of the Committee having expressed *"doubts as to the wisdom of seeking to bring over large numbers of coloured men for war work in this country ... serious difficulties, for example with accommodation and health"*, decided to import unskilled workers from the West Indies for training for the munitions industries.[67]

1942

Lord Moyne seized the opportunity provided by Labour's proposal to the Lord President. Together with Ernest Bevin, Minister of Labour, he renewed the demand for West Indians to be used as pioneer units in the Middle East. The War Office consulted the Middle East Commander-in-Chief, who again rejected the West Indians on the same grounds as before, ie, that West Indians employed at British rates of pay working alongside Indians and West Africans at substantially lower rates of pay would be bound to cause trouble; and he did not want to use shipping for West Indian instead of British troops. (The Commander-in-Chief's previous rejection of the West Indians has not been preserved in the Public Records Office.)

Despite the Commander-in-Chief's refusal, because of the combined pressure from the Minister for Labour and the Secretary for the Colonies, the War Office had to reconsider the use of West Indians. The Adjutant General prepared a memorandum for the Executive Committee of the Army Council meeting held on May 22, 1942. The paper summarised all the previous correspondence and stated the current position as:
1. British manpower shortage was acute
2. the British Honduran Forestry Unit has stood up to the British climate
3. the West Indian colonies want to participate in the war
4. it would be difficult to provide British officers and non-commissioned officers, but it might be possible to find some in the colonies

5. it would be difficult to provide shipping
6. West Indians would have to be additional to the Army's authorised ceiling of numbers
7. large numbers of West Indians may cause difficulties especially as there might in the near future be large numbers of US negro troops in Britain
8. British troops and Auxiliary Territorial Service might want higher pay than West Indians
9. at the end of the war there might be political pressure from the West Indian Governors for the men to be demobilised in Britain.

Another submission to the meeting, by *"C.M."* stated that the Army Council could not be expected to *"accede to a demand for employment in the UK of several thousand West Indians purely on non-military grounds and because of political considerations affecting the West Indies"*. But because the manpower shortage was so acute, if shipping could be found, perhaps the West Indians could be considered for the Middle East.[68]

At the meeting itself, the Adjutant General said that there was *"heavy political pressure"* regarding West Indians. There were about 200 of them in the Army already; some had come as individuals and there were a *"small number of fitters doing good work in the Middle East, although a somewhat larger number had not proved satisfactory in the Royal Engineers, possibly owing to being given unsuitable employment in the Corps"*.[69] The Army Council agreed that because of the manpower shortage, West Indians might be desirable. However, as there were difficulties regarding accommodation and shipping, the only decision they could reach was to again reject the use of West Indians even as labour units. Individual skilled tradesmen would continue to be acceptable.

1943

The correspondence between the War Office and the Colonial Office for 1942 has not been preserved. From the one remaining file for 1943, it is obvious that the Colonial Office, despite the May 1942 rejection, continued to press the War Office to revise its decision. In a letter dated April 20, Mr Brind, writing on behalf of the War Office, found some new excuses: special reinforcement provisions would be necessary; if casualties were not replaced, a West Indian corps would not be a viable unit. There was also the problem of there being other non-European troops in the Middle East, at lower rates of pay. Mr Brind suggested the possibility of garrison duty in Madagascar, Ceylon or Burma. Mr Holt pointed out in his reply that the pay disparity would be the same everywhere; that it was politically important to find an *"outlet"* for the West Indians and that the continuing gross manpower shortage made it very difficult to explain away the War Office's continued refusal to accept West Indians.

Brigadier A.E. Stokes-Roberts, Commander-in-Chief of the South Caribbean Area, also asked the War Office why, in view of the manpower shortage, were West Indians not recruited? In his letter of 24/3/43, he suggested that those whites in the West Indies who were not employed in industries vital to the war effort should be conscripted if they were not willing to volunteer. He also suggested *"selective conscription"* of the *"coloured population"*, who, *"provided they are officered by a high percentage of British officers will acquit themselves on active service just as well as many units of the Indian Army or troops from East or West Africa"*.[70] He therefore recommended that a contingent should be raised — this would raise West Indian morale and improve esprit de corps. There is, unfortunately no copy in the file of the War Office's reply to Brigadier Stokes-Roberts.

In July, the War Office again reiterated that they did not want the West Indians; however, *"the door is left open in case at any time the present shipping difficulties can be overcome"*. By August, Colonel Stanley, now Secretary of State for the Colonies, had a new Caribbean problem to content with. He explained in a letter dated 9/8/43 to Sir John Grigg, Secretary for War, that the Americans were about to send Puerto Rican troops to Trinidad, St Lucia and British Guiana; West Indians would not accept Puerto Ricans as white (irrespective of how the Puerto Ricans saw themselves) and would wonder why they are seen as so inferior that alien Blacks are needed to garrison their own islands. (Stanley had tried unsuccessfully to prevent the US sending Afro-American or Puerto Rican troops to the Caribbean islands. The Americans, equally unsure about men from their colonies, preferred to send Puerto Ricans on garrison duty.) It was essential, Stanley emphasised, that West Indians should be sent to an active theatre of operations.

Within a couple of weeks, the Colonial Office received an outcry from the Jamaican Governor: the US was proposed to send Puerto Ricans to Jamaica as well as Antigua, while Jamaicans were not even trusted to protect their own island which was garrisoned by Canadians and Britons. But the War Office was adamant, and even managed to find new excuses as well as repeat all the old ones for not recruiting West Indians: West Indians were not a robust race; special administrative staff would be required and there would be complications with pay; as a thousand West Indians would have to be deducted from the Army's monthly intake ceiling of 4,000 and as the West Indies could furnish neither officers nor tradesmen, the Army would in fact be losing; the only way shipping could be found would be to replace US troops with Caribbean troops and the permission of the Combined Chiefs of Staff would have to be sought. Though the War Office conceded that they could see the political problems, especially as the US was intent on using Puerto Ricans in the Caribbean, they already had *"a fairly formidable racial problem on their hands. It has taken infinite patience and forbearance on all sides to maintain good relations with the Americans in the face of the coloured question . . . and our efforts have not met with unqualified success . . . The introduction of a further racial problem seems to me to be asking for trouble."*[71]

Colonel Stanley replied point by point: there was absolutely no evidence that West Indians were not *"robust"*; he did not understand why they would have to be counted against the monthly intake as they would not be part of the British Army; the shipping problem was not really so serious now; the suggestion was not for the West Indians to be brought to Britain, but to be sent to North Africa. He suggested that the Prime Minister should be asked for a ruling.

Sir John replied on December 17: because of the political reasons, the War Office was now prepared to consider using West Indians, not as labourers, but for garrison duty which might lead to an active theatre of operations. He warned that it should be *"remembered that in the last war West Indians were employed in a combatant role in Palestine where they proved quite unsuitable and caused considerable trouble"*. Aircraft artillery was another possibility, but this required six months' training and *"their staying power under aerial bombardment is untried and suspect"*. They could possibly be used in Italy or North Africa as an infantry garrison unit, and it might be possible to avoid using the word 'garrison' in their title.[72]

The one other remaining file for this year is the only one preserved dealing with women recruits. When the Governor of Barbados complained to the Colonial Office that the visiting Controller of the Auxiliary Territorial Service said that only *"girls of pure European descent"* could be recruited, Mr Mayle passed on the complaint to the War Office in a letter dated January 30. Lt Col W.E.G. Williams, the Assistant Adjutant General, replied on March 20: *"We are prepared to accept any European girl ... but we cannot agree to accept coloured women for service in this country"*. After some discussion, at the end of March the War Office agreed to *"enrol British West Indian women into the Auxiliary Territorial Service for service with the British Army staff in Washington, and for local service in Jamaica and Trinidad"*. The War Office suggested that their decision should be discussed at a meeting with the Auxiliary Territorial Service and the Colonial Office. The minutes of this meeting, held on April 2nd, state that it was decided to issue a *"charter, covering both Washington and the Caribbean, though in practice only white women would be selected for Washington ... the Colonial Office representative stressed that this fact should not be recorded in the Recruiting Officer's charter. It was essential that this discrimination should appear a matter of* selection *(emphasis his) and not of racial distinction."* During April the Governors and the Commanders of the North and South Caribbean Areas were duly informed that *"There will be no repeat no colour discrimination in arrangements for enrolment, but for your information, no coloured women will be sent to Washington."*[73]

Though all the letters have not been preserved, it appears that on the basis that there were some Black women in the Auxiliary Territorial Service in England, Colonel Stanley took up the issue of discrimination against Black West Indian women with the Secretary for War. On May 3, Sir John Grigg wrote arguing that the Black women in the Auxiliary Territorial Service were probably resident in Britain before they joined; on the 12th, Stanley replied that if the War Office was not prepared to accept Black women they should not recruit whites either. On May 19 Sir John conceded that though he did not like Stanley's *"ATS ideas; [as] my people say that they can manage up to 30 in this country without discomfort and as, from what Gater says, this will satisfy you, I will agree. But I don't like it . . .*"[74] The 30 'coloured' and 30 white women whom Grigg agreed to accept arrived in England by the end of the year. From the incomplete material available, it appears that Black women were never employed by the British General Staff office in Washington, because they "might cause embarrassment to the American authorities". Despite a brief note among the internal memoranda in CO968/81/4 that the US employed Black ATS in Washington, the Colonial Office was obviously satisfied with the token gesture made by the War Office and did not take the issue any further.

1944

Stanley's suggestion that a West Indian corps should be used in North Africa was taken up, and the matter went to the Cabinet for decision. At its meeting on January 6, 1944, the Cabinet decided that 1,000 West Indians should be recruited with contingents from all the major islands.

The Royal Air Force, having decided in 1943 that it would recruit ground crew and trades trainees in the West Indies, began testing applicants towards the end of the year. By April 1st the deficiencies in ground crew numbers were estimated to be 58,000; 3,985 West Indians arrived in Britain between June and November to help fill this gap.

1945

In March 1945 the final contingent of 1551 ground crew recruits for the RAF arrived in England.[75]

In February the War Office asked the Commander-in-Chief in India to accept the Caribbean Regiment, which was by then undergoing training in Jamaica. Despite repeated requests, the Commander-in-Chief refused to accept the Caribbeans. The Regiment was then offered to Field Marshall Alexander for garrison duty in Italy; Alexander did not want them either, and proposed guard duty on German prisoners of war in the Middle East, but this was thought unsuitable. Having run out of options, the War Office decided that the Regiment, now undergoing final training in the US, would have to be returned to the West Indies. On learning this from cables marked 'Secret', the Governors protested, and probably under severe political pressure the War Office relented. The Regiment was allowed to sail to Italy, where it underwent further training; in September it sailed for Egypt, underwent more training, played cricket and sailed home in the *Highland Monarch* on December 22. According to Mr Sabban-Clare of the Colonial Office, who visited Egypt with the Duke of Devonshire, then Under Secretary of State for the Colonies, "*Colonel Allfrey, Commander of the British troops in Egypt, spoke disparagingly of the West Indians . . . General Nye also said he had a low opinion of them. There is no doubt the Caribbean Regiment have had the dice loaded against them all the time. The War Office didn't want to take them out of the West Indies and the Commanders who received them were equally unwilling . . . General Allfrey said that administratively they present a difficult problem since although nearly all of them are coloured, they wish to be treated exactly as white troops.*"[76] One can only wholeheartedly agree with the note scribbled by Mr Beckett in the margin of Sabban-Clare's report: "*In other words, the Army are colour-bar minded*".

The Colonial Office, not satisfied that the Inter-Departmental Committee on Demobilisation had sufficiently emphasised to all the Services the decision which had been reached in October 1942, that colonials should not be demobbed in the UK, talked with the Air Ministry about the issue. As an official in the Ministry minuted: "*on strong representations made verbally by the Colonial Office it was arranged . . . that no airman who had come from overseas . . . should be allowed to receive his discharge in the UK.*"[77] The 1942 reasons for this decision had been that the Committee were "*alive to the serious social consequences which might arise from the demobilisation in this country of any appreciable numbers of certain classes of coloured men . . .*" The Committee had considered asking for legislation to ensure that "*coloured men*" could be deported but had "*been assured that the possibility of such legislative action has already been given very full attention, and that there are strong political and administrative objections to such a course as the men are British subjects*".[78]

However, for reasons I have not been able to discover, the men were demobilised in Britain. The *Crown Colonist* on page 832 of the December 1945 issue, while noting that West Indian Royal Air Force ground crew had not been used outside the UK, stated that "*Steps are being taken to discourage West Indians from attempting to profit by offers of casual employment in Britain. It will be pointed out to them that repatriation at Government expense will apply only for a stated period and that those who disregard the warning and stay in Britain will be thrown upon their own resources . . . In this way it is hoped that what might become a major problem will be avoided."* One major problem faced by those who accepted repatriation was lack of shipping: according to Philip Noel-Baker, Secretary for Air, those 1000 or so men still awaiting repatriation in March 1947 were expected to depart during the following months.[79] About 2000 men from the RAF remained in Britain after the war, taking further and higher education courses under the resettlement schemes.

1982

It has not been possible to discover the armed forces' policy towards Blacks today; the Ministry of Defence say they do not have such information. A member of staff at a Military College has written to me saying *"I don't think you will find any statistics in respect of the present day, I'm afraid. I know of three or four non-white officers (of Indian or East African Asian origin). There are numbers of black soldiers in regiments such as the Fusiliers and the Queens that recruit in areas with a high immigrant population; also a number in the Artillery and in the two medical corps. Also a number in the WRAC. It seems to me they have an equal chance of becoming NCO's and certainly very many do."*[80]

Footnotes and references

1 Committee on Post War Regulations Respecting the Nationality and Descent of Candidates for the Army; in the Minutes of the ECAC meeting, 16/3/45, in WO 32/10592.
2 Note by the Secretary of the Principal Personnel Officers Committee, in Minutes of the ECAC meeting 27/4/45, ibid.
3 Internal memorandum by Mr Lee, 14/10/39, in CO 323/1673.
4 Winston Churchill to Malcolm MacDonald, 16/10/39, ibid.
5 Circular telegram to all colonial governors, 24/12/39, ibid.
6 Memorandum from the CO to the War Cabinet, 6/1/40, WP(R)(40)6, in CAB 68/4.
7 'British-born' and 'British subject' were then interpreted as meaning born in the UK. Britain has, since the 16th century, manipulated the meaning of these phrases according to whether or not 'colonials' were needed in the armed forces, the merchant navy or labour in the UK.
8 Malcolm MacDonald to Harold Moody, 4/12/39, in CO 323/1672.
9 CO to the Air Ministry, 7/3/40, and the Air Ministry's reply, in CO 323/1729 (1940).
10 Hansard, 24/1/40, vol 356, cols 562/3.
11 Internal memorandum by MacDonald, 16/4/40, and CO to Farrell (Admiralty), 23/3/40, in CO 323/1801.
12 Nationality Rules Regarding Entry, in ADM 1/10418.
13 Circular telegram to all colonial governors, June 1941, in CO 820/4.
14 War Office to Lord Moyne, 2/12/41, in CO 968/38/10.
15 Correspondence re VADs, October/November 1941, in CO 968/38/11; *The Scotsman* advertisement reported in the LCP's *Newsletter*, January 1942; report on the ARP, October 1939, in CO 323/1692 (file 7213/2); Hansard, 23/9/43, vol 382, col 390.
16 All quotations from the LCP's *Newsletter*, January and July 1942.
17 Foreign Office Circular, W 3004/1695/49, 26/3/42, in CO 968/134/3.
18 Correspondence in CO 968/13/3. It is very rare to find a Ministry admitting that the units from the West Indies were a success; it is even more rare to discover an official admission that the units were segregated. See my *Forestry Unit in Scotland*, 1941-43. Section III.
19 Correspondence, ibid. In September the Dominions Office did ask Canada, on behalf of the Office, to accept West Indians into the forces and as civilian labourers. The Canadian Government replied that there were no openings in the RCA or the RCN; neither was civilian labour needed. Men would, however, be accepted for the Army, provided they paid their passage to Canada, passed the medical examination and paid for their own repatriation on discharge. After objections from the DO, in June 1943 Canada accepted responsibility for repatriating discharged West Indians. According to the Canadian Directorate of History at the Dept. of National Defence, the total number of West Indians in the Canadian forces was 247. I think that is an underestimate, but I have not been able to investigate further.
20 Internal memoranda and correspondence in FO 371/350519.
21 W L Rolleston (CO) to the War Office, 4/12/42 and further correspondence dated 16/3/43, 31/3/43, 25/6/43, 22/11/43, 20/1/44, in CO 820/50/36065.

22 ECAC Meeting 6/8/43, ECAC/M(43)32, para 190, in WO 163/74. It is interesting to note the depths of jingoism in the army. In the WO32/10592 the Director of Staff Duties, Major General J S Steele minuted on 10/2/43 that "We should like gentlemen of North American, Australian or New Zealand Descent (as officers) but do not want those descended from various types of European parents even if they themselves are British". Obviously to the DSD anyone with British ancestry was superior to anyone else.
anyone else.
23 Correspondence in FO 371/43005.
24 Once conscription had been introduced, the army found it impossible to reject Black recruits. It has not been possible to ascertain from the Ministry of Defence the numbers accepted. Most of the Blacks in the RAF were from the West Indies. I have not been able to discover if any British Blacks had been accepted by the RAF.

It is instructive to look at the machinations of the Admiralty, as revealed by the few remaining files, a little more closely. In 1939 the Secretary of State for the Colonies assured Churchill, then First Lord of the Admiralty, that he would be quite prepared to co-operate in preventing Blacks from seeking entry into the Navy, but he felt that "from the political point of view, we should be able to say that there are no regulations debarring" Blacks from being eligible for entry into the Navy. (MacDonald to Churchill, 10/10/39, in ADM/110818.) Churchill agreed and informed the Admiralty staff. The First Sea Lord, Admiral of the Fleet Sir Dudley Pound, noted that "in practice much inconvenience would arise if this theoretical equality had many examples...I cannot see any objection to Indians serving in HM Ships...But not too many of them please...". (Memorandum dated 14/10/39, ibid.) It was therefore decided that "Indian gentlemen can be given temporary commissions in the Royal Naval Reserve for the duration of the hostilities". (CW 21276/39, ibid.)

RN recruiting staff were informed that British-born Blacks with British-born parents on both sides could henceforth be accepted as volunteers for the duration of the war. Recruiting officers were asked to file a separate weekly return for Black volunteers. (DNR99, dated 15/3/40 in ADM1/14149.) These separate returns have not been preserved at the PRO and the Ministry of Defence's Naval Historical Branch could not trace them for me. The Ministry of Labour, in charge of National Service registration, was informed of this decision, and was asked to "mark 'C' on the papers of all 'coloured' national servicemen". (Admiralty to the Ministry of Labour, 28/3/40 in ADM1/10818.)

In 1943, when the King's Regulations were revised, the Naval Recruiting Regulations still stated that "black and coloured boys and any person in whom there is evidence of such parentage or ancestry are absolutely ineligible for entry unless with special sanction of the Admiralty". Though the First Sea Lord, the Director of Naval Recruiting and the Director of Personnel Services had concurred that there was to be no discrimination, the files do not indicate that the Regulations were changed until 1948. (AFO P150/48, dated 2/4/48.) Even then Black candidates had to be referred to the Director of Naval Recruiting before acceptance, which presumably meant that in practice Blacks continued to be excluded from the Navy.
25 Minutes of Air Council meeting, 3/10/44, in AIR 6/75.
26 Colonial Office: Paper on Nationality and Descent, ECAC/M(44)48, in WO 163/95.

27 Paper by Principal Personnel Officers, ECAC/M(44)48, ibid.
28 Minutes of ECAC meeting, 1/12/44, ECAC/M(44)48, ibid.
29 War Office to the Colonial Office, 4/12/44, in WO 163/95.
30 Col. Stanley to Sir J Grigg, 27/2/45, ibid.
31 Report of the Committee on Post War Regulations Respecting Entry to the Army, ECAC/P(45)28, in WO 163/96.
32 Report, op cit.
33 Report, op cit.
34 Report, op cit.
35 Minutes of the 11th Air Council meeting, November 1945, in AIR 6/75.
36 Correspondence between Lord Stansgate and George Hall in WO 32/10598.
37 Letters from the Admiralty, 18/12/45, and the Minister for War, 23/1/46, ibid.
38 Minutes of the 64th meeting of ECAC, 12/4/46, ibid.
39 Minutes, op cit.
40 ECAC's Paper for the Cabinet, CP(46)271, in CAB 129/11.
41 The Admiralty's Paper for the Cabinet, CP(46)293, ibid.
42 Paper by the Secretaries of State for India and for the Colonies, CP(47)154, ibid.
43 Brief for the Secretary of State by the Army Council Secretariat, 27/7/46, ACS/B/2104, ibid.
44 Paper for the Cabinet by the Secretaries of State for India and for the Colonies, 16/5/47, CP(47)154, in CAB 129/19.
45 Paper for the Cabinet by the First Lord of the Admiralty, 16/5/47, CP(47)155, in CAB 129/19.
46 Brief for the Secretary of State by the Army Council Secretariat, 21/5/47, ACS/B/2366, in WO 32/10592.
47 Cabinet decision re the removal of the colour bar, 3/6/47, CM(47)51, in CAB 128/10.
48 Report on the Colonial Empire by the Secretary of State for the Colonies, Sept. 1939, WP(R)(39)7 in CAB 68/1.
49 Cabinet decision regarding West Indian manpower, 25/1/40, WM23(40)3, in CAB 65/1.
50 Report of the meeting held at the War Office 28/9/39 (AG1 BM B/108), in CO 363/1673.
51 Report on the Colonial Empire, 5/10/39 in WP(R)(39)31, in CAB 68/1.
52 Circular telegram to all colonial governors, 24/11/39, in CO 363/167.
53 Report on the Utilisation of Colonial Manpower, by the Secretary of State for the Colonies, 22/1/40, WP(G)(40)15, in CAB 67/4.
54 The West Indian Regiment dates back to the American War of Independence. Though not allowed to serve as combatant troops in Europe as it was "against British tradition to employ aboriginal troops against a European enemy" (quoted in W F Elkins, The Revolt of the British West Indies Regiment at Taranto, Italy, *Science and Society*, vol 33, no 2, 1970), the Regiment served "with credit" and "did excellent work" in East and West Africa. The British West Indies Regiment of 15600 men was raised towards the end of 1915. This Regiment served in Egypt, Palestine, Mesopotamia, France and Italy. The men in the two regiments were awarded 5 DSOs, 9 MCs, 8 DCMs, 37 Military Medals and 49 Mentions in Despatches. (CO 363/1673 and CO 323/1672.) However, the BWIR mutinied against their treatment and conditions: being used solely as labour corps, no promotion beyond NCO level, unequal pay, segregated facilities and racialism; "several men died from sheer neglect in No

43

; Native Labour Hospital . . . In every theatre of war where West Indians were employed, they were to a great extent the victims of colour prejudice", according to Lt. Col C Wood-Hill's *A Few Notes on the History of the British West Indies Regiment*, privately published in 1919. This, coupled with trouble in the holding camps in England while the men waited for long months for repatriation at the end of the war, is far more likely to have been the basis of the Colonial Office's recommendation and the War Office's attitude towards the West Indies. (The West India Regiment was disbanded in 1927; the BWIR had only been raised for the duration of the war.) See also N G Holdich, Military Forces in the West Indies, *The Sprig of Shillelagh*, vol XXVIII, no 326, 1950, and B G Baker, The West India Regiment, *The United Services Review*, March 9, 1939.

55 Letter from West Indian firms, 31/1/40, in CO 318/445.
56 CO to the Governor of Trinidad, 25/5/40, in CO 323/1801 (file 13117/16).
57 The Governor of Trinidad to the CO, July 1940, ibid.
58 The Governor of Jamaica to the CO, 29/5/40, in CO 323/1801 (file 13117/2c).
59 The Ministry of Air to the CO, 11/11/40, in CO 323/1729 (file 2244/1d).
60 Bigg of the CO to the Air Ministry, April 1949, in CO 323/1828.
61 It has not been possible to discover how many men from the West Indies had been accepted by the Army as skilled tradesmen. Though I have the names of at least 35 who served with the Royal Engineers in the Middle East, the RE's librarians and historians have disclaimed all knowledge of these men.
62 The Governor of Jamaica to the CO, 12/2/41, in CO 968637/10.
63 Minutes of the ECAC meeting, 2/5/41, ECAC/M(41)13, in WO 163/72.
64 Telegram from the Governor of Jamaica to the CO, 7/10/41, in CO 968/37/10.
65 As the High Commissioner for Canada explained to the Dominions Office in a letter dated 4/11/41, Canada turned down the offer of Jamaicans because of "prejudice against Jamaicans which could lead to embarrassing difficulties . . .The Canadian Army is most unlikely to allow coloured men to obtain commissions". (CO 968/38/5.) The Canada West India League, in a letter to the West India Committee in London dated 22/12/41 expressed their belief that the UK High Commission might well have obstructed their plan to co-operate with various organisations in the West Indies attempting to help West Indians enlist in the Canadian Army. The League's suspicions seem to be confirmed by a letter from the High Commissioner to the DO asking for clarification for the Canadian Government as to whether the UK agreed to West Indians joining the Canadian Army. On May 14, 1942, the DO replied that there was no policy decision yet; but in July the DO informed the High Commissioner that as all UK plans for the "further utilisation of West Indian manpower" had been abandoned, there were no objections to West Indians enlisting in the Canadian armed forces (CO 968/74/15).

Lt. Col. K B Jacobs, of the Canadian National Defence Medical Centre, informed me in a letter dated 1/12/82 that "There were indeed segregated units (in the Canadian armed forces) during WW1. Very early in WW2, there were local recruiting unit attempts to exclude not only Blacks but people of other races. . . All of this changed in the face of a nationally enunciated policy which was the result of either political pressure, attrition or perhaps both." J Walker in *Identity: The Black Experience in Canada* (1979) maintains that Blacks were never accepted by the Canadian Air Force and Navy, and that though the Army enlisted

Blacks, "the stereotyping persisted: they were enlisted as cooks, barmen, orderlies, etc".
66 Meeting of the Lord President's Committee, 19/12/41, in CO 968/37.
67 188 skilled workers had been imported by the Ministry from the West Indies during 1941. A further 332 unskilled men arrived in Britain during 1942. See Section II.
68 Note by 'CM' in ECAC/P(42)66 in WO 163/88. I have been unable to discover the identity of CM.
69 Minutes of ECAC meeting no 60, 22/5/42, in WO 163/88.
70 Brigadier Stokes-Roberts to the WO, 24/3/43, in CO 968/17/5.
71 WO to the CO, 23/9/43, ibid.
72 Sir J Grigg to Col Stanley, 17/12/43, ibid.
73 Circular telegrams, 7 and 22/4/43, in CO 968/81/4.
74 Sir J Grigg to Col Stanley, 19/5/43, ibid.
75 Out of a total of approximately 6347 men and 78 women from the West Indies who served in the War, about 811 men were aircrew.

Neither the aircrews' nor the groundcrews' experience of life in the RAF was free from racial problems. According to an internal memorandum in CO 537/1223 dated 16/3/44, "some of his brother pilots said quite openly that they refused to sleep alongside a coloured man... Such expressions of opinion were not uncommon". The Air Ministry's official report, Manpower Contribution of the Colonies to the RAF 1939-45, in AIR 20/1022, on page 5, says: "a large proportion of the coloured ground personnel were not happy in their life in the RAF, owing to faults by no means entirely on the coloured man's side . . . The employment of both aircrew and ground personnel was affected by the colour of their skin . . . The attitude of . . . certain of the Dominion forces precluded the employment of coloured RAF personnel in RAF Overseas Commands, and in Transport Command in the case of aircrew, nor could they be used in India because of the possible effect on the RIAF airmen attached to the RAF, who were paid at lower than RAF rates". On page 28 the report admits that "the colour bar, tacit or open, put immeasurable checks on the organisation and employment of the enormous manpower potential of the Empire".
76 Memorandum by Mr Sabban-Clare, 11/4/45, CO 537/1266.
77 Note by the Air Ministry, 17/3/43, in CO 968/78/9.
78 From the draft for the Minutes of the Second Report of the Inter-Departmental Committee for the Machinery for Demobilisation, RP(42)33, in CO 968/78/13.
79 Philip Noel-Baker, Minister for Air, replying to a question, 25/3/47, Hansard vol 435, col 190.
80 When in 1968 E J B Rose enquired about 'coloured' recruits in the RAF and the Army, the RAF replied that such statistics were not kept. The Army replied that there were 2,087 in the ranks, of whom 859 were NCOs. The Army had no figures available for Black officers. One must presume that Rose did not even think it worth while to ask the Royal Navy if they had 'coloured' ratings. (E J B Rose, et al, *Colour and Citizenship*, London, 1969, p.306.)

2. West-Indian Munitions Workers in Britain 1941-45

INTRODUCTION

The Under-Secretary of State for the Colonies, Lord Lloyd, addressed the peoples of the British Empire in a broadcast on October 15, 1940: *"The Empire is one of the glittering prizes which tempted the gangsters of the Axis* (who) *had declared that the war would be the test which would expose the rottenness of an Empire only just held together by a shrewd mixture of farce and commercial interest. . . . The importance of the Colonies is strategic, economic . . . and the provision of manpower. . . . The Colonies thus return to their early role of strategic defenders of noble causes. . . . In the provision of manpower there is a vast reservoir hitherto untapped . . ."*[1]

From the British West Indian viewpoint Lord Lloyd's words must have sounded particularly hollow. The only 'cause' the islands had ever been called upon to defend was slavery — not much nobility in that. Glittering prizes? The Royal Commissioners, sent to the islands subsequent to the 'disturbances' which spread throughout the area from 1934 to 1938, concluded that *"The social services in the West Indies are all far from adequate for the needs of the population, partly as a result of defects of policy, and largely through the paucity of the funds at the disposal of the Colonial Governments which are in the main necessarily responsible for these services. In education there is a great need for more teachers, better-trained teachers, more and better school accommodation and equipment, and curricula more closely related to the life and experience of residents in the West Indies. Health conditions, though better than in some other British Colonies, are unsatisfactory, and much of the ill-health arises from poverty and ignorance. Medical departments are handicapped by lack of funds, and far more attention has generally been devoted to the cure of disease than to its prevention. The diets of the poorer people are often insufficient and usually ill-balanced, although nutritious foods of all kinds necessary for health can be produced without much difficulty in almost every West Indian Colony. The reason for this appears to lie fundamentally in the divorce of the people from the land without the provision of compensatory arrangements which would help to ensure adequate food supplies for the displaced population. Housing is generally deplorable, and sanitation primitive in the extreme, although sporadic improvements are being effected as well by Government as by private interests. There is in general, no balanced farming system capable of maintaining soil fertility at a high level and of ensuring proper interplay of crops and stock. Especially on peasant holdings the soil tends to be exhausted and rendered liable to irreparable damage by erosion. Really efficient agriculture is almost entirely confined to estate cultivation of sugar, where careful and thorough methods have enabled yields to be maintained and enhanced even without rotation or resting of the land. Conditions of land tenure militate against good husbandry by peasants. Rents are high in relation to yields, tenure is uncertain, and is sometimes on the basis of share-cropping.*

"So deeply entrenched in West Indian agricultural practice is production for export, and consequent concentration on a single crop, even among peasant proprietors, that the necessary development towards food production on the basis of mixed farming constitutes practically an agricultural revolution."[2]

The shine on this glittering prize was obviously a little too tarnished: it is therefore hardly surprising that on receiving the Report in January 1940 the Prime Minister felt that *"the German Ministry of Propaganda would seize on this information . . . neutral countries might be turned against the United Kingdom"* and decided to suppress the Report.[3] [a]

There certainly was a 'vast reservoir of untapped manpower' in the Caribbean, but the British government refused to open the sluice gates until the war was almost over. During the first four years of the war the only Caribbeans recruited were a few air-crew for the RAF, some 700 lumbermen to work in Scotland, and 350 men for munitions work in the North-West of England. By examining the government's files at the Public Record Office I have attempted to discover why there was such reluctance to employ West Indians in the war effort. Many government files have been destroyed and those government officials still alive whom I have managed to trace have all replied to my letters claiming that their memories are too hazy and unreliable to comment on my enquiries. What emerges from the remaining files is a picture of

[a] WM(40)27, CAB 65/5

racism and racial prejudice throughout the ranks of British society: Black men were not wanted in Britain even in times of crisis.

That such a degree of racial hostility should have manifested itself against such a few men and at a time of national crisis when all other willing hands were welcomed, demonstrates the emptiness of the current argument that it is either the economic recession or the vast numbers of Blacks presently in Britain that evokes racism and racialism. A cursory glance through contemporary journals and newspapers would demonstrate that the small numbers of Black people resident in Britain during the first 40 years of this century experienced a considerable degree of racial discrimination, and that the ideology of racism was prevalent in the English mind. Economic recession only heightens the already existing attitude which culminates in calls for the deportation of British citizens. There have been increasing calls for repatriation during the past three years, as there were for the deportation of the war workers in 1945/6 and as there was in 1925 when by means of the Special Restriction (Coloured' **Alien** Seamen) Order the government succeeded in deporting hundreds of **British** unemployed seamen by the simple expedient of instructing the Chief Constables, charged with implementing the Order, to *"register all coloured seamen"*. [a]

Why, given these racist attitudes, did HMG import *any* West Indian workers? Even the International Labour Office queried the economic viability of the West Indian workers when balanced against the expenditure on the special segregated hostels and the numbers of welfare staff employed. The answer must lie in the emphasis the Colonial Office always laid on the political importance of being seen to be doing something to alleviate the worsening conditions in the West Indies. Offering work to 350 men for the duration of the war (the foresters, also supposedly employed 'for the duration', were repatriated after two years in Britain) is the most miserly of token gestures. But even such a token allowed the Colonial Office to claim that it was doing something, that West Indians were being used in the war effort. The Colonial Office had, after all, to provide HMG with a means to answer possible criticism from Britain's allies, from colonial governors and possibly from the Americans, who, the Prime Minister felt in 1940, were *"at the present time very much on the*

[a] HO45/11897

lookout for items of information that were damaging for the British case".[a] Perhaps the *"rottenness of the Empire"* was indeed *"only just held together by a shrewd mixture of farce and commercial interest"*, and it was the Colonial Office's job to keep this well hidden.

The conflicting interests and attitudes of the various government departments regarding the Empire and colonial workers shows clearly in the files. Of course, all were concerned, to a greater or lesser extent, with maintaining the ideology of Empire: white was right, had the might, and the Black man had to be kept in his allotted place. The only differences lay in how each department put this ideology into practice. Of the three departments most closely involved with the Black workers in Britain, the Ministry of Supply, as evidenced by their behaviour towards both the munitions workers and the lumbermen in Scotland, were the most rabidly racist: they obviously thought that Blacks were barely human and acquiesced with protestations and with calls for greater and greater disciplinary powers to the men's presence in Britain. The Ministry of Labour, bowing to pressure from their Minister Ernest Bevin, who clearly saw the need to placate the Caribbean islands and to deflect possible American criticism, accepted Black workers in a half-hearted fashion and certainly raised no objection when deportation was discussed. The Colonial Office, whose job it was to keep the Empire under control, had, therefore, not only to control the men but also to provide them with some semblance of care in order to prevent complaints of their treatment in the UK stirring up the peoples of the islands. The Colonial Office thus had to attempt to exert pressure on other government departments to behave as decently as possible towards the men. This was not an easy task and not one entered into wholeheartedly by all Colonial Office staff.

Though the efforts of the League of Coloured Peoples, and the Colonial Office and Ministry of Labour welfare officers must not be discounted, that the West Indian workers succeeded in making a 'small but significant' contribution to the war effort despite the odds being so heavily weighted against them is a considerable achievement. Through their own efforts, through their powers of perseverance, their skills, their adaptability and their determination to overcome the obstacles placed in their path the men demonstrated the lie of all the racist aspersions cast on them.

[a] WM(40)27, CAB 65/5

THE DECISION TO IMPORT WEST INDIAN WORKERS

In September 1939 the Colonial Office reported to the Cabinet that an *"intense wave of loyalty was sweeping through the British West Indies"*;[a] but the Governor of Jamaica cautioned that *"this may not be maintained unless suitable openings can be found for utilising the numerous offers of service for military and other duties"*. Other West Indian Governors echoed this warning. A month later, presumably in an effort to appease and ensure the loyalty of the Empire, it was announced in Parliament (October 19) that the colour bar in the British armed services would be lifted **for the duration of the war** (my emphasis). However, this did not mean that the Government intended accepting Blacks into the services: the Colonial Office sent secret telegrams to all the Colonial Governors on 24 December 1939, telling them that *"it is not desired that non-European British subjects should come here for enlistment"*.[b] The Foreign Office advised its Consular offices on 10 November 1939 that *"only offers of service from white British subjects should be considered"*.[c] The Colonial Office informed the Cabinet on 6 January 1940 that their decision had been put into effect: *"Colonial Governments have already been informed that it is not desired that non-European British subjects should come here for enlistment"*.[d] How to handle the contradiction was left to the Governors' discretion. This was the policy throughout the war as both the Colonial and Foreign Offices admitted: for example, a Foreign Office memorandum of February 1944 stated: *"we must keep up the fiction of there being no colour bar while* (actually) *only those* (Blacks) *with special qualifications are likely to be accepted"*.[e]

The Colonial Office found itself in a dilemma: the West Indian Governors were having to cope with chronic un- and underemployment, with the memory of recent 'disturbances' (agitation

[a] CAB 68/1
[b] CO363/1673
[c] CO363/1673
[d] CAB 68/4
[e] FO 371/43005

for a living wage, the acceptance of trade unions, for workers' compensation, decent housing, education, etc., which swept through the British West Indies during 1934-38) and with pressures from new indigenous political parties and trade unions. The outbreak of war revived memories of the shameful treatment of the British West Indies Regiment during World War I, when the Regiment was used as a labour corps and not as a fighting unit; ex-servicemen's invalid pensions were still being disputed by HMG in the '30s; and the proposed settlement of ex-servicemen on arable land had seldom been carried out. However, the population had to be kept loyal to the Mother Country and propaganda to this effect was increased.

Having whipped up enthusiasm without providing a means to satisfy the craving for military honours and glory, what were the Governors to do? By the end of 1939 the Governors were already pressing His Majesty's Government to raise troops in the West Indies; some advocated fighting units, others pioneer (labour) units. Accordingly, the Colonial Office approached the War Office with the idea of resuscitating the West India Regiment, and stressed the political importance of using West Indians in the war. But the Colonial Office did not envisage fighting troops: their aim, as stated in an internal memorandum dated 11 September 1939,[a] was *"to raise units which, while nominally military units in the proper sense of the term, would actually be employed on duties somewhat analogous to those performed by labour battalions"*. The War Office turned down the offer of West Indian troops/ labour — and continued to turn it down until the end of 1943 when recruiting began for RAF ground-crew trainees and men for the Caribbean Regiment which, though shipped overseas, was kept in enforced idleness in Egypt until the end of the war.

Meanwhile, material and social conditions in the Caribbean worsened. Because of the war, the thousands of workers who annually sought contract work in and around the territories of the Caribbean Sea, in the Panama Canal Zone and in the USA, had to return home. Submarine activity prevented the export of produce and the importation of the basic foodstuffs (rice, flour, salt-fish and meat) on which the colonial system had forced the population to depend.[1] Where local food production was increased, the shortage of petrol prevented its distribution. The lack of shipping and

[a] CO323/1672

the fuel shortage in turn led to increasing unemployment in the waterfront and transport industries. There was some amelioration of this situation while the United States required labour to build its bases in British Guiana, Trinidad, Antigua, St Lucia and Jamaica, but this was short-lived except in Trinidad. By the last quarter of 1942, the US layoffs at all the other bases were adding a vociferously discontented group to the ranks of the unemployed. Men who, however briefly, had enjoyed the steady wages and huge amounts of overtime paid by the Americans found it very difficult to accept being jobless again. Although 4,000 were unemployed in Barbados by April, the situation was most serious in Jamaica whose Governor reported in December 1942 that 150,000 to 200,000 people were un- or underemployed. And, by mid-1942, the cost of living had increased by 46% throughout the islands. In 1943, doubtless to prevent a new outbreak of rioting on its doorstep during the war, and also to fill the gap in its agricultural labour force created by general mobilisation, the US began recruiting agricultural labour in Jamaica. In 1944 recruitment was extended to Barbados. A total of 48,619 Jamaicans and 939 Barbadians worked in the US from 1943 to 1945. Approximately a thousand Bajans were directly recruited and 4,851 Jamaicans transferred from agriculture to the US War Manpower Commission for work in industry.[2]

Britain, on the other hand, was suffering from a serious manpower shortage which grew steadily worse as the war progressed. For instance, the War Cabinet was informed at their meeting on 6 January 1942 that 40,000 workers were required for foundry work, 30,000 for engineering, 24,000 for coalmining, 17,000 for agriculture and 20,000 for motor mechanics. From early in the war, women, school children on vacation and prisoners of war were used to augment the industrial and agricultural labour force.

So great was the labour shortage that early in 1940 the Ministry of Agriculture approached the Colonial Office with a request for labour from the West Indies. But the Colonial Office was not enthusiastic: *"although a number of West Indian labourers would have agricultural experience, it was with agriculture of an entirely different kind"*, they wrote. *"The men would not be used to the working conditions of this country. From the employers' point of view they would probably be found unsatisfactory. In addition there are many other points such as questions of health and morals which would have to be taken into consideration. . . . There are more POWs in South Africa and India who could be brought over"* [a]. The Ministry of Agriculture accepted the Colonial Office's racist assumptions about the West Indians' working prowess, health and morals without question, and the matter was dropped until March 1942 when B. Riley, MP for Dewsbury, raised the issue in the House of Commons. The Minister for Agriculture replied that the whole question of bringing West Indian civilian labour to the UK was being considered. A month later the *"question was still being considered"*. In July 1943 D. Adams, MP for Durham, asked in the House of Commons why, if West Indian labour was suitable for US agriculture, could it not be used in Britain? The Secretary of State for the Colonies, Colonel Stanley, was evasive in his reply: the question had been raised a number of times, he said, but agricultural work in the West Indies was *"too different"* from agricultural work in the UK; in any case, shortage of shipping prevented the importation of either agricultural or unskilled workers. The excuse of shortage of shipping was used by both the Colonial Office and the War Office on a number of occasions when the employment of West Indians for either civilian or military purposes was discussed. But, as will be shown, when for political or other reasons the West Indians were needed, shipping was always available. Thus token groups of workers were brought to Britain in 1943; RAF ground crew recruits began arriving in June 1944, and the Caribbean Regiment was shipped to Italy in July 1945.

There were people in the West Indies clamouring for an opportunity to aid the Mother Country's war effort (and, as well, to find work), and the Governors pointed out to the Colonial Office that the use of foreign labour in Britain while men in the British West Indian colonies were becoming unemployed in increasing numbers was becoming a source of resentment and discontent. The Colonial Office was thus forced into forwarding Jamaica's June 1940 offer of 2,000 men for the *"motor and mechanical industries"*, whose passage to the UK and return home at the end of the war would be provided by the Jamaican Banana Producers Steamship Company. The Ministry of Labour replied *"that there was a large pool of under- and unemployed labour with mechanical aptitude in Britain. . . . The Ministry does not consider it would be advisable to introduce into this country*

[a] LAB13/37

workmen who have only an elementary knowledge of mechanics and would require to be trained and accommodated in special establishments". Why they thought Jamaicans were necessarily untrained or needed special accommodation the Ministry's letter does not divulge. *"However"*, their letter continued, *"there is a marked shortage of toolmakers, tool setters, coppersmiths, fitters and turners, draughtsmen and instrument makers . . . fully skilled persons could be utilised . . . at rates of pay and under conditions applicable in this country . . . the AEU would expect any such workmen to become members of the appropriate union . . ."*.[a] The Ministry was obviously quite unfamiliar with conditions in Britain's colonies if they thought they could obtain *"fully skilled draughtsmen and instrument makers"* from the British West Indies; skilled fitters, turners and coppersmiths were, however, available.

While this correspondence was being carried on between the Ministry and the Governor of Jamaica via the Colonial Office, the newly appointed Labour Adviser in Jamaica wrote independently to the Ministry: *"One thing I would like to do, which I think would help you on your side as well as mine, is to export to England some of the skilled mechanics who we have here and who could be spared without difficulty"*. Once the breach of protocol committed by the Labour Adviser in writing directly to the Ministry rather than via the Colonial Office was sorted out, this suggestion was accepted: the Munitions Labour Department needed skilled men; the Treasury agreed to pay the men's passage; the Amalgamated Engineering Union agreed to the scheme on condition that the men joined the Union. The Labour Adviser was cabled the existing pay rates and told that passages would be paid by HMG; it was thought, however, that *"these wages would probably be sufficient to attract men without the necessity of paying lodging allowances (of 24/6d per week) which are payable to men here transferred to work away from home"*. (As the Ministry had previously told the Colonial Office, they hoped to *"avoid paying the lodgings allowance"*.)[b] The Labour Adviser accepted the terms and set about recruiting men.

Despite these negotiations, the Colonial Office remained unhappy about importing Black colonials into Britain and continued to press for their use outside Britain. In a Note for Cabinet

[a] LAB8/65   [b] LAB13/37

discussion on manpower on 19 December 1940, the Colonial Office wrote: *"the West Indies are the main colonial source, so far hardly touched. Large numbers are available for our war effort and are only too anxious to be given a chance. They would be most suitable for pioneer units."* But, as discussed previously, the War Office did not want to enlist West Indians and the Colonial Office had to settle for the token employment of a few Black colonials in UK factories.

RECRUITMENT

The first two contingents of 117 Jamaicans arrived in February 1941. They were destined for the Royal Ordnance Factories and other munitions works in the North-West region where, the Ministry and the Colonial Office had decided, they could be *"absorbed"* most easily. After all, Merseyside had had a 'coloured' population for generations and hence the people and the employers must be used to living and working alongside Blacks. It would be interesting to know if this decision was based on ignorance, which would be difficult to believe, or on the hope that given the documented difficulties Blacks in the area historically faced, the *"experiment"* of importing even a small number of West Indian workers would prove a failure and hence no more would need to be brought to the UK.

M. E. Fletcher's questionable 1930 *Report on the Colour Problem in Liverpool*[4] showed that Blacks in the area lived in a ghetto and that *"there was little likelihood of employment for coloured men"* (p. 14). Investigating the chances of *"half-caste juveniles"* being offered employment, of 119 firms she wrote to, 63 did not reply and 45 said they would not employ them. *"Several employers who would otherwise have been willing to give coloured juveniles a trial said they were afraid to do so as the white employees would object to working with them"* (p. 33). Ten years later M. Caradog Jones's survey of 225 'coloured' families found *"only 40% in receipt of any earnings"* (p. 15) and 28.9% living at least 10% below the poverty line.[5] *"Anglo-negroid children when grown up do not easily get work or mix with the ordinary population"* (p. 75)[6]; the unemployment rate of 21% given by the Juvenile Employment Bureau was most likely an underestimate, Jones wrote. In 1942 Major Orde Browne acknowledged that *"some regret must be felt that Liverpool was of necessity the centre for employment for these men; the selection of some other city, without the evil background and traditions of Liverpool would have avoided much trouble*".[a]

Probably because of the difficulty in finding employment for the Jamaicans, early in 1941 the Ministry informed the Colonial Office that *"for the time being, we feel that we do not want any more men from Jamaica or the West Indies until we have gained more experience of the way the first two batches settle down"*. The Colonial Office replied on 29 March 1941: *"In the Colonial Office we hope that it will be possible to continue the scheme. To close down on it now would certainly make unfavourable impression in the West Indies. We would not press* **the political considerations if on other grounds further recruitment is found to be more trouble than it is worth, but we should be grateful if you would bear them in mind as important...**" (emphasis mine). An internal memorandum in the Colonial Office noted that the *"selection of the men had been hasty and inefficient"* and that the question of bringing over more West Indian artisans was uncertain, *"largely because of the attitude of the AEU"*. Whether, in fact, the selection had been 'hasty and inefficient' is doubtful, as *The Gleaner*, the Jamaican daily paper, reported on January 3rd that there was *"a very satisfactory response to the call for skilled engineers for Great Britain . . . 250 skilled men registered by January 2 . . . A fairly high percentage of the men who passed the practical test also got through the medical test. But of course there was a fairly high percentage who failed the practical test due to the fact that the Kingston Employment Bureau is ensuring that only first rate men are selected.*" The truth of the matter probably lay in the fact that under the colonial system with the inherent lack of opportunity for apprenticeship or technical education, and the lack of capital investment in modern machinery, it was not generally possible for a Jamaican to attain the level of competence reached by the best of British craftsmen. Neither, of course, were there any factories in Jamaica where the men could have gained industrial experience.

Within a month the Ministry apparently acquiesced to this pressure from the Colonial Office. In May the Colonial Office telegrammed the Governors of British Guiana and Jamaica that another 200 skilled artisans would be welcome. A final group of

[a]CO876/46

71 Jamaicans, but no Guyanese, arrived at Merseyside in August 1941 and were dispersed amongst the Royal Ordnance Factories (ROFs) and local factories.

The Director of the Jamaican Banana Producers Association, Mr Williams, who had accompanied the men from Jamaica, put a new proposition to the Colonial Office: couldn't Britain use some of Jamaica's unemployed dockers and unskilled young men? The offer of dockers was immediately turned down, but the Colonial Office's new Secretary of State, Lord Moyne, forwarded the proposal to Ernest Bevin, the Secretary of State for Employment, in a letter dated 3 September 1941: *"You will shortly have placed before you a proposal to bring over from the West Indies a certain number of young men for training for the munitions industry. . . . I ask that you will give this proposal a very sympathetic reception and approve it if you can. . . . For political reasons, I attach great importance to the proposal. The people of the West Indies are eager to take an effective part in the war effort but so far it has not been possible to give them much opportunity, and there is a danger of the spread of a sense of frustration and 'unwantedness'.* **Anything that we can do to give the West Indies a part in the war effort is of the utmost political value locally . . ."** (emphasis mine). Bevin replied on September 11: "*. . . I will bear in mind particularly the considerations you put forward . . ."*.[a]

However, Mr Grundy, the Ministry's senior official in the North-West, where it was planned the men were to be trained and employed, was not very keen on taking Black workers,-despite a shortage of 160,000 workers in the area. Grundy wrote to the Ministry's Headquarters on September 20 that *"the men couldn't be absorbed in Liverpool and the Merseyside"*; Headquarters replied: *"I am surprised at this decision in view of the shortage in your region"*. Grundy tried again: *". . . the West Indians should be particularly suitable in drop forging and non-ferrous metals industries . . . the work is heavy and hot . . ."*. Perhaps what Grundy had in mind was the recent report by Major Orde Browne, Special Adviser on Colonial Labour in the Colonial Office, on West Indian and West African workers on Merseyside, which stated that *"West Africans find suitable work in the preparation of Trinito-toluol, as the dark pigment in the skin apparently confers a large measure of immunity from the rash and other symptoms liable to afflict white*

[a] LAB18/83

workers handling this explosive".[a] But Headquarters was adamant: *"It would mean labouring work rather than jobs for which training would be required"*, they wrote. Eventually Grundy had to give in: *"We require these men for the North West"*, he conceded on October 13. Ernest Bevin obtained *"the approval of both sides of the engineering industry"* and wrote to Lord Moyne that as he needed *"all the men I can get to be trained for munitions work I shall be very glad to have these young men from the West Indies."* The Lord President Committee's advice, that West Indians should not be brought to Britian because *"there would be serious difficulties, e.g. with accommodation and health"*, was overruled.[b] The Governors were advised of the scheme on December 16; a quota of 50 men each from Jamaica and Barbados and 20 each from British Honduras, the Bahamas, British Guiana and the Windward and Leeward Islands was proposed. After some debate between the Colonial Office and the Ministry, it was decided that though it would hardly encourage recruitment, the terms and conditions sent to the Governors should include the *"appallingly heavy income tax under which we labour in the UK"*.[c] However, the usual 3 to 5 month training period in the GTCs was not offered to the West Indians: they were to undergo a basic training course of 4 to 8 weeks; *"appropriate"* trainees were to be given the opportunity of a maximum of 16 weeks' training. The Colonial Office did not object to this discrimination.

All the Governors except Trinidad's, where all the available labour was working on the US bases, replied that many more men than the quota allocated to them were available for the scheme. The quotas were therefore proportionately increased and by the end of 1942 332 men had reached Britain, despite one Barbadian group being torpedoed en route. (Five men were killed and most of the remainder of the contingent either stayed in Bermuda to work on the docks or returned home.)

[a] CO876/46
[b] CO968/74/15
[c] CO968/38/3

RECEPTION AND ORIENTATION

Recognising the political importance of arranging for the reception of the men, the first group was greeted with much ceremony. The 51 men who landed in Methil in Scotland on February 15 1941 were welcomed by a Ministry and a Colonial Office Welfare Officer, and the Provost of Methil. They were then bussed to Edinburgh where warm overcoats, one suit and two hats were supplied to *"those men needing them"*; the use of ration, identity and unemployment cards and gas masks was explained. The day after their arrival the men were registered at the Employment Exchange, received gas masks and the necessary cards, as well as an advance of £1. The Senior Magistrate and the Controller for the Ministry of Labour officially welcomed the men to Scotland; in the afternoon they were taken on a bus tour of Edinburgh; the following morning they were put on the train for Liverpool. On arrival there, the Lord Mayor welcomed them yet again and a telegram of welcome from the Secretary of State for the Colonies was read out; the following morning the men were sent out to their employers.

The second group of men arrived in Liverpool on February 25 and were quite unceremoniously allocated to employers on the evening of their arrival. They were expected to commence work the following morning. The third group of Jamaicans arrived in August and were at least provided with temporary housing in the newly ready West Indies House. However, the clothing allowance was reduced to 25/- plus a boiler-suit. The files reveal nothing further about this group's reception or that of the eight groups of trainees who arrived in Britain between June 1942 and January 1943.

Apart from ceremony, nothing was apparently done to help the men acclimatise to the northern winter or to foreign working conditions and environment. The unions only decided some time after their arrival to address the men. Prospective employers and foremen were not informed of the men's very different life and work experience. Though they could hardly have avoided awareness of racial prejudice in Britain, and especially in the Liverpool area, at this stage neither the Colonial Office nor the Ministry attempted to do anything to counteract this.

HOUSING

During the war, people who had to work away from home were housed either in hostels or billeted in private homes. Obviously, similar arrangements should have been made for the West Indians — but weren't.

Admittedly Merseyside had been heavily bombed and accommodation was hard to find; nevertheless there seems little excuse for the first arrivals being 'housed' in the Birkenhead YMCA's gymnasium. The second group were offered emergency accommodation by the School for the Blind in Wavertree. Eventually the Harold House Boys' Club in Liverpool was taken over, renovated and renamed West Indies House: some permanent and temporary accommodation was thus available from August '41. By mid-1942 there were three government hostels in the Liverpool area and one each in Manchester and Bolton; all were segregated. A few — less than 20 — Jamaicans reamined in the YMCA, which was 'mixed'; between 150 and 200 men were housed in the segregated government hostels and the remainder in private lodgings.

The Bolton hostel, a fine mansion set in gardens on the outskirts of the town, and under the direct control of the Colonial Office, does not appear to have experienced any problems. The Manchester hostel also seems to have been trouble-free. Major Orde Browne visited the hostel, which was formerly a YMCA hostel: he found *"conditions generally probably far better than the young men had previously experienced at home"*. Despite this presumption, he noticed that there was no method of heating many of the rooms and asked that this be remedied before the onset of winter. There was still no heating and no electricity in these rooms by the end of January 1943.

The situation in Liverpool was radically different, especially in West Indies House at 91 Chatham Street. While under the management of the YMCA, there were constant problems: the police were called in a number of times and the men had complained to the League of Coloured Peoples about this, and conditions and restrictions. One resident wrote: *"because of the colour bar that exists in Liverpool the staff feel they are doing us a great favour.*

Because we are black we were not treated as humans".[a] Despite the men's complaints, by the time the third group of technicians arrived in August 1941, *"West Indies House was functioning as a reception centre for all the men on arrival ... in spite of many drawbacks and many deficiencies the House is serving a good purpose. Over 40 men board there and others use it as a social club"*.[b] The Colonial Office, investigating the 'drawbacks', found a *"certain amount of trouble in internal management"*; thought the *"premises not satisfactory"* and that *"difficult problems of management remain to be solved"*.[c] Losses, attributed to breakages caused by the men's carelessness and the wastage of food resulting from the men working varying shifts, amounted to £1,000 in a three-month period. The Colonial Office decided to take over the management and a new warden was installed in October 1942. However, P. G. Macdonald of the Colonial Office, visiting the hostel at the end of the month, found an *"atmosphere of discontent and unrest... the new warden Mawson unsettled and harassed ... internal organisation leaves much to be desired ... discipline not satisfactory ... some of the residents difficult"*.[d] Both Learie Constantine and Rudolph Dunbar, a Guyanese journalist then working for the Ministry of Information, agreed that there were some undesirable residents. However, a note by Mr. Leggett of the Ministry indicating that two men, previously considered *"trouble makers"* had settled down and were causing no further problems since moving to new jobs, as well as the men's complaints noted above, perhaps illuminiates the causes underlying *"difficult behaviour"*.

Another new warden was appointed, but to no avail. It was reported to the April 6, 1943 meeting of the Advisory Council for the Welfare of Colonials in the United Kingdom that the *"position continues very unsatisfactory ... the neighbourhood of the street is not very desirable ... two men causing dissension ... problems will not be solved until the undesirable elements have been weeded out and sent home"*. It was suggested that the hostel should be moved to a more suitable and less *"institutional"* building in the suburbs; however, as this would be very expensive, perhaps the hostel should just be closed down. But that would be admitting defeat and give rise to bad publicity, and might incidentally cause problems to the men who would be made homeless. It was noted

[a] LAB26/52
[b] CO859/76
[c] ACWUK 16/9/42
[d] ACWUK Oct 1942

that the Ministry of Labour was attempting to repatriate the unsuitable men; the Colonial Office decided to persevere.

However, when the Ministry attempted to deport the men, even going to the length of asking the police to hand them their letters of dismissal and repatriation, the men refused to go, claiming that as they were British subjects they could not be deported.

Whether for reasons of bad management, a bad neighbourhood, the unsuitability of the building, the staff's racism, or a few men's difficult behaviour, the situation in the hostel did not improve. A resident was stabbed; the police were called in a number of times. In May, 1943 Professor Mary Blacklock of Liverpool (who had been a member of the Moyne Commission), wrote to Sir George Gater at the Colonial Office, asking that something be done about the hostels; she claimed that some of the wardens and domestic staff had been assaulted and asked for some *"higher authority"* to maintain discipline. Dr. Blacklock also wrote to the Secretary of State for the Colonies voicing her concerns. Sir George contacted Mr. Leggett at the Ministry, whose reply indicated that arrangements were in process for either repatriating the men or having them called up for national service. Though we know that neither of these ruses for getting rid of the men worked, we have no further information about life at this hostel.

In fact, there is almost no information about what life was like in any of the hostels. Major Orde Browne, who visited them all, noted a lack of books and other recreational material. He also commented that *"English diet was proving quite acceptable to the Honduranians* (the Manchester hostel residents), *in spite of their pronounced dietetic peculiarities at home; they accept normal meals readily"*.[a] The Major's racist statements, at least regarding food, are contradicted by a Ministry note dated December 1942 which commented that *"there was still trouble over food"*.

Apparently at least one of the ROFs which employed the men had hostels attached to it: Constantine wrote that when the *"hostel dwellers objected to coloured residents, I went to live there myself, hoping that the white workers could see that I was an ordinary person like themselves and then might be willing to try some coloured people.... Actually the ruse proved quite successful"*.[7]

[a]CO876/46

Those men who did not wish to live in hostels experienced considerable difficulty in finding landladies willing to rent them rooms; they were frequently overcharged and treated as curiosities. For example, one man reported that his landlady invited the neighbours to tea to meet *"her niggers"*. The usual excuse given by landladies for refusing to let rooms was that neither their husbands not the neighbours would condone living with *"coloureds"*[8]. When attempting to rent flats, negotiations were conducted either in writing or by white wives.

EMPLOYMENT

As employment had not been arranged in advance for the men, the Ministry of Labour's 'good' intentions towards them are questionable: in fact, the Ministry's Welfare Branch had to *"take steps to break down the colour bar that had existed in a number of places"* in order to secure jobs for the men.[a] On many occasions the 'steps' they took were not successful despite the chronic labour shortage, and many men experienced periods of unemployment. According to Learie Constantine, who was employed by the Ministry as a special Welfare Officer for the West Indians, *"some firms either flatly refused to take on coloured men, or put endless delays in their way hoping to make them seek work elsewhere"*.[c]

The Ministry's original plan, to send all the men to Napiers Aero Engine factory, had to be abandoned because of racism: Napiers refused to take the men *"partly on grounds of colour and partly on the ground of their alleged unsuitability"*.[b] Even when employed *"Black workers (were) considered with a certain degree of hostility by their white colleagues; chargehands and foremen (were) not very tactful in handling difficult circumstances"*, Superintendent Gale of Royal Ordnance Factory Kirkby reported to the Ministry on 21.11.41.[d] Mr. Keith of the Colonial Office found *"the position of those in private firms not satisfactory.*

[a] LAB25/52
[b] LAB13/37
[c] Constantine, p147
[d] LAB26/35

Some of them are in garages or are employed by the Bolton Corporation and so forth. I have made representations to the Ministry of Labour about this. . . . Some private firms on Government work refuse to take coloured people on the pretext that workers would not work along with them."[a]

The men who were brought to the UK for training at the Government Training Centres also experienced difficulty in finding jobs, and again the cause was racism. Mr. Watson, the Ministry's Senior Welfare Officer in the North-West with special responsibility for the West Indians, investigated the refusal by De Havillands to take 28 GTC trainees in February 1943. He was told that though the 17 Bahamians already employed there were satisfactory, it was felt that the addition of another 28 black workers to the total labour force of 6,000 would be "*too many colonials*". The white workers felt that the "*Jamaicans*" had been given preferential treatment by being sent for GTC training; they should be employed on the lowest rated unskilled or semi-skilled work, at labouring wages, in any case, the men would walk out at lunchtime if the Colonials came to their factory. Mr. Watson pacified the men by offering them the possibility of GTC training and eventually agreement was reached to accept the 28 men. However, it was thought prudent to place the "*further 15 allocated to De Havillands elsewhere*".[b]

It also appears that at least some of the GTC trainees were not accepted as even semi-skilled workers when placed in employment. Mr. Watson in May 1943 was considering sending some men back for further training as he had found them doing unskilled work: "*some of the men feel* (their) *work* (is) *routine and repetitive*" he noted.[c]

[a] Report 31/11/41, CO859/76
[b] LAB26/56
[c] LAB26/56

EMPLOYMENT: DISPUTES

Racism was also a major factor in the problems the men faced concerning work disputes and promotion. There were serious disputes at the Royal Ordnance Factories at Kirkby and Fazakerley. As a result of complaints by both West Indians and West Africans of their *"general treatment, unhappy atmosphere and lack of courtesy and co-operation"*, Mr. Cummings of the Colonial Office's Welfare team and Mr. Constantine went to discuss the problems at Kirkby with Superintendent Gale on October 23, 1941. As mentioned above, Mr. Gale admitted the hostility of whites towards Blacks and went on to say that it was *"quite true that both African unskilled and West Indian skilled workers did far more work than their white colleagues. ... This has something to do with the resentment felt for them by white workers."* (It seems the Black worker is always in the wrong: if he doesn't work 'hard enough' he is lazy; if he works 'too hard' he is resented.) Mr. Gale's proposal to appoint two workers' representatives, one African and one West Indian, to participate in the resolution of disputes was accepted. Four months later, in February 1942, the representatives were eventually appointed and admitted to the factory's Whitley Council. However, when Mr. Cummings visited Kirkby in February he found that though Mr. Hyde, the West Africans' representative, was working full-time as a welfare officer, he was not officially called that, his labourer's wage had not been increased and he had not been given an office. For Mr. Pringle, acting as the West Indians' representative was an extra duty. The factory's Welfare Department had not bothered to inform the managers, foremen, etc. of the appointment of Messrs. Hyde and Pringle and thus they were not always asked to attend disciplinary hearings. The Ministry's representative at the ROF substantiated Mr. Cummings' claim that *"the management take no proper steps to hear both sides when a West Indian or a West African employee is accused of misconduct"*. As a result of pressure from the Colonial Office, Messrs. Hyde and Pringle reported in June 1942 that *"things were improving"*, and the factory's management conceded that Mr. Hyde's *"work was of great value"*.[a]

[a] CO876/44

We have very little knowledge of the disputes the men must inevitably have been involved in. Lord Constantine mentions one: *"In one area, a number of coloured workers came out on strike because one of them had suffered unpleasant discrimination. I settled that and got them to go back — but then the white workers said they would strike if these coloured men came back without suffering financial punishment for causing an illegal stoppage. I settled that, too, in the end — some cricket gossip did it, as far as I can recall."*[a]

EMPLOYMENT: DISPUTES RE PROMOTION

There were similar problems at the Royal Ordnance Factory in Fazakerley. In August 1942 the men wrote to the Superintendent listing their complaints; disciplinary problems; lack of promotion; being called *"niggers and coolies"*; foremen who *"make it their duty to instruct operators not to speak to us"*.[b] The Superintendent replied to the men on 14.8.42: *". . . The promotion of an operative even to the lowest rank, even of a temporary nature, has an implication which is difficult to appreciate. The individuals so promoted attain, even if only to a small degree, a status which the majority of those already holding these positions feel is only compatible with British born nationality. It would, for instance, be, for me equally difficult to sanction such a promotion to a citizen of the US of whatever race, as it would to a similarly racially descended individual who was a native of the West Indies. . . . You have my assurance that, with the above reservations, there is no bar to the advancement from a monetary point of view to any individual in this work."*[c]

Not satisfied with this obscurantist but clearly racist reply which promised nothing but the possibility of working overtime, the men asked the League of Coloured Peoples (LCP) to take their complaints further. Dr. Moody, the LCP's chairman, visited Fazakerley early in 1943 and detailed his findings to the Ministry: there was a total absence of promotion; some foremen and assis-

[a] Constantine, p147
[b] LAB26/53
[c] LAB26/53

tant foremen acted in a discriminatory manner; unfounded charges against West Indians sometimes ended in a verbal apology which was not felt to be real compensation.[a] Probably as a result of Mr. Moody's intervention, Mr. Riley, MP for Liverpool, asked a question in the House of Commons regarding the lack of promotion among West Indian workers. Though Mr. Riley stated that he had a letter from the manager in one of the Royal Ordnance Factories in his constituency saying that he (the manager) will not promote but would be willing to increase wages, Sir A. Duncan, replying on behalf of the Ministry of Supply, claimed that there was *"no colour bar in this matter whatsoever"*.[9]

By 1943 the Ministry was well aware of the reluctance to promote black workers. In July 1942 J. J. Taylor of the Ministry admitted in a letter to Mr. Creech Jones, MP, that *"it does not follow that in every case white workers would willingly accept coloured foremen, even though some of these men have all the qualifications of good foremen"*.[b] In December of the same year Mr. Harris, Deputy Director General of Ordnance Factories, explained to the Ministry that the lack of promotion was due to the *"fear of the Superintendents that the promotion of coloured men would cause resentment among white workers"*.[c] Nevertheless, in October 1943 after *"a protracted struggle to get one of the West Indians promotion at this ROF"*, V. M. Dunckne was promoted to foreman at Kirkby and two other men were promoted to charge-hand. There is no record of any promotions at Fazakerley, nor were Black workers' representatives appointed there.

Doubtless in order to be seen to be combating this aspect of discrimination the Ministry set up foremanship training courses for West Indians in Manchester and Liverpool in 1944. Though the Principal reported that *"the average intelligence of the students was well up to that of the usual British students on similar courses"*, passing the course does not appear to have resulted in promotion for any of the students.[d] And there is no explanation given as to why West Indians had to attend segregated courses.

The files do not contain complaints by West Indians of similar discriminatory practices in the private firms where they worked. The refusal of Napiers to employ Jamaicans and the reluctance of De Havillands to take more than 17 Black workers

[a] LAB26/56
[b] LAB26/52
[c] LAB26/53
[d] CO876/76

has already been noted. The Shell Co., in June 1941, wanted to dismiss all 40 West Indian employees on the grounds that they would not be able to work outdoors in the winter and because *"fellow workers object to the Jamaicans' personal habits"*.[a] It is hardly likely that the West Indians' experience in private firms was different from their experience in the Royal Ordnance Factories. The silence of the files on this can probably be attributed to the fact that though the Colonial Office had asked the Ministry to keep the men together in units they ended up scattered among 50 employers up and down Merseyside. Neither the Ministry nor the Colonial Office had enough staff to monitor the progress of men so widely dispersed.

EMPLOYMENT: PRAISE AND COMPLAINTS

Throughout the men's stay in England there were intermittent complaints about them, such as being incompetent, lazy or unskilled, as well as some praise. Investigating some of these complaints, the Colonial Office found, for instance, that absenteeism at Metropolitan Vickers had been the final outcome of men being temporarily laid off due to *"hitches in production"*.[b] Reduction in the amount of overtime available and wages lower than those being paid at nearby factories led to reduced output *"in order to gain discharge in order to gain better wages at the higher paying factories"*.[c] Even a Labour Officer at an unnamed ROF, while complaining of absenteeism (and not accepting the men's explanation that they had trouble adjusting to the English climate), admitted that the men were of *"a good type; in fact several of them are, in many respects superior or even much better educated than the majority of English workers"*.[10]

Within a few months of employing them, in March 1941 ICI told the Ministry that they found the West Indians *"very useful and excellent material for training for more skilled work"*; they would happily take more *"West Indians of similar quality"*. At the same time the Ministry reported that *"the more skilled men who*

[a] CO859/76
[b] CO323/1863
[c] CO876/46

were placed with the ROFs appear to be giving satisfaction".[a]

In October 1942 Major Orde Browne, reporting on a tour of inspection of the *"West Indian Artificers"*, wrote of the group training in Manchester: *"those in charge of them in all cases spoke highly of them and they seem to have made a good impression both for behaviour and for capacity and anxiety to learn ... (they) appear to make progress as good as, if not better than the equivalent European"*.[b] A month later the Ford Motor Company, the Hondurans' employer, wrote to the Ministry that they *"were quite anxious to take another group of men of like quality"*.[c]

In January 1943 Mr. K. Richards at ROF Kirkby received a £5 prize for an invention which *"improved efficiency"*.[d] In March 1943 despite the earlier problems and Mr. Cummings' observation that though conditions had improved there were *"distinct signs of resentment from the white men in the employ of this firm"*, De Havillands asked the Ministry for more West Indian labour.[e] In the same month the North-West Training Committee reported on the GTC trainees: *"the men had been satisfactorily trained and those placed in employment are giving satisfaction ... (they) have been a useful contribution to the war effort"*.[f] At the end of the year an International Labour Organisation inspector visiting the 30 men working at De Havillands found them *"doing semi-skilled work requiring a high degree of care ... the men were recognised as capable workers. Some of the top grade finishing work was being done by West Indians."*[g]

It seems therefore that despite racialism, distrust and discrimination, the West Indians rapidly adjusted to working conditions in wartime England and became successful workers. This achievement must be seen in the context of the men's earlier work experience in the West Indies: the climate there is warm and sunny the year round; employment is often seasonal or temporary; standards of craftsmanship and trade demarcation lines were less rigorously and mechanically defined than those obtaining in English factories. Many of the men, especially those from rural areas, might well not have had any contact with white people and hence with white racialism. It must also be remembered that though many Englishmen did not see their families until they were granted home leave, the West Indians were separated from their families and the familiarity and comfort of their homelands for years.

[a] LAB13/37
[b] CO876/46
[c] LAB26/52
[d] LAB26/53
[e] LAB26/53
[f] LAB18/97
[g] LAB18/97
[h] CO876/48

UNIONS

As stated earlier, the Ministry of Labour was careful to obtain the blessing of the Amalgamated Engineering Union before agreeing to the importation of Black workers. However, the AEU's agreement either did not percolate down to the local level or the Ministry had not fully acquainted the Union with the conditions of craft-training in the Caribbean. On 14.3.41 the Ministry was forced to write to the AEU about the West Indians: *"your local representatives on Merseyside have shown some hesitation about accepting them without evidence that they have served a full seven years' apprenticeship. As you will appreciate, conditions in the West Indies are not the same as over here . . . I believe you could accept them, at any rate for the duration of the war, in some class of membership."* The AEU bowed to the Ministry's request: *"my Executive Council have considered this question and have issued instructions to our Liverpool District that these men be enrolled into membership of this Union"*, they replied on 1.4.41.[a]

The Boilermakers' Union apparently raised similar objections to West Indian membership, as Mr. Watson remarked in 1942 that he was *"still negotiating with this Union over the issue of apprenticeship"*.[b]

How successful either the AEU's instructions or Mr. Watson's negotiations were is open to question as one of the craftsmen at ROF Kirkby complained to the Ministry early in 1942 that *"we do not join the union; I and others make an application and give it to the foreman and he says they do not accept us . . ."*. Given these problems regarding union membership, it is not surprising that when Major Orde Browne visited the Merseyside workers in September 1942 he noted that *"there appears to have been some failure to pay Trade Union subscriptions promptly, and complaints from the branch Secretary have been met with general levity"*.[c] The Major's opprobrium at this behaviour ignored the fact that the West Indians had little experience of the benefits which could be derived from unionism and, given the unions' reluctance to accept them, the men must have doubted if these benefits would ever be extended to them. As the International Labour Organisation, investigating the experience of the West Indians in Bolton, reported

[a] LAB13/37
[b] Watson, p8
[c] CO876/46

in November 1943 that the *"position regarding the AEU is not finally settled ... the central problem is the apprenticeship issue"*, the men's levity was probably well justified.[a]

The only information we have of other unions' attitudes is from Mr. Constantine: *"some of the Unions were very difficult to deal with, the Boilermakers' Union for instance. ... The electrical Unions, on the other hand, were most helpful, and allowed coloured representatives to take places on Union Committees"*.[b] Despite these difficulties, Richmond reported that of the 180 craftsmen, 148 had joined unions; of the 129 trainees, 50 were union members.[c]

It is a sad reflection on the chauvinism of the trade unions that this issue over apprenticeship did not alert them to the problems of labour in the British West Indies. There is no evidence to indicate that at any time they brought pressure on or even questioned the government regarding the lack of industrial training in the Caribbean or the non-recognition of unions by the West Indian colonial governments.

WELFARE

The Ministry of Labour obviously recognised that special measures had to be taken to look after imported workers. Arnold Watson was appointed *"2 or 3 days before the men's arrival to make adequate arrangements for the men, not only at the reception point, but also throughout their stay with us"*.[d] The Ministry did not enlighten Mrs Watson as to how he was to make 'adequate' arrangements of any kind two days before the men's arrival. Learie Constantine, the famous West Indian cricketer who was living in Lancashire at the outbreak of war and working in a solicitor's office preparing to get articled, was asked in May 1942 to accept a position as Welfare Officer for the West Indian workers.

These two men, with support from the Colonial Office's welfare department which was set up in May 1941, had to tackle a vast spectrum of problems: as mentioned earlier, there were

[a] CO876/48
[b] Constantine,p147
[c] ibid,pp67-8
[d] Watson,p2

problems with accommodation, hostels, unions and employers; problems with racism; problems with remittances the men were sending home and with sick pay. Though there were also personal problems, most difficulties clearly arose because the dominant community was reluctant to treat Black workers as equals.

Besides these official efforts, the League of Coloured Peoples frequently intervened with officialdom on the men's behalf. The League also arranged holidays in London for small parties of workers. The Colonial Comforts Fund, under the auspices of the Colonial Office, provided books, magazines and radio sets for the hostel common rooms. On rare occasions sick men were given small grants from the Fund. The Victoria League and the Over-Seas League also offered hospitality to men on leave who were sometimes invited to official receptions at the Colonial Office.

WELFARE: SICK PAY

In April 1941 the Ministry noted that they were still trying to deal with the Colonial Office's complaint that the West Indians were not eligible for sick pay during their first six months in the UK.

Given the change in climate from tropical to temperate, unaccustomed and wartime diet, and the long hours worked by the men (the ILO reported an average of 70 per week), there must inevitably have been illness, especially during the first few months after arrival. This ineligibility must therefore have had very serious consequences for the men and could only have been made in total disregard of the men's welfare. We do not know how the issue was resolved.

But the problems over sick pay did not end there. The ILO noted in November 1943 that the West Indians' contract specified *"special payment . . . in lieu of wages"* if the men were ill. The workers believed that they should therefore be *"entitled to subsistence"* whereas Ministry officials interpreted this clause as *"assistance will be given if need is proved"*.[a] The ILO officer asked for urgent reconsideration of this; whether his request was carried out we do not know.

[a] CO876/48

WAGES AND REMITTANCES

From the day of their arrival the men were concerned for the welfare of their families left behind in the West Indies. Richmond relates how the men allocated to one of the Royal Ordnance Factories in February 1941 refused to work when they discovered that the wage rates were lower than the rates indicated to them in Jamaica. The men asked the Ministry official sent to deal with them *"how it would be possible for them to live on these rates and to send money home"*. The official suggested that overtime and production bonus would help and undertook *"to represent their case in London"*, whereupon the men said they would start work the next day. *"Hurried negotiations with London led to the establishment of a special expatriation allowance of £1 per week, which, it was subsequently arranged, would be paid directly into an account for them in the Colony"*.[a] The men's protest that this was still less than the living-away-from-home allowance of 24/6d being paid to English workers did not succeed in increasing their allowance. (The YMCA charged 27/6d per week to temporary and 30/- per week to permanent residents.)

The men's initial complaint that they were not being paid the wages indicated to them in Jamaica as being the rates for *"skilled workers in G.B."* was wholly justified. Presumably in order to attract the men in the first place, the rates quoted by the Ministry to the Labour Adviser in Jamaica were those being paid by Napiers, who paid the highest wages in the North-West. Wages and the availability of overtime and production bonuses varied from factory to factory and men with similar qualifications in the same factory could be put on jobs with different wage rates. These differentials were an endless source of grievance and caused frequent job changes as the men sought to improve their wages. According to Richmond, by October 1944 *"a total of more than 50 employers had employed one of more West Indians"*.[b]

The problems over remittances grew rather than decreased, especially for the Jamaicans. As there was some delay before the men could begin sending money home (the length of the voyage to UK, dispute over wage rates, etc.), various voluntary bodies in Jamaica stepped into the breach and subsidised needy families; in

[a] Richmond, p38
[b] Richmond, p41

some cases 10/- per week was paid to dependants by the Jamaican government from the Charitable Vote. Problems arose over who constituted 'family', over the amounts to be paid to various claimants, and over the demand for reimbursement by the voluntary bodies once remittances began to arrive. According to Mr. Keith's Report of 13.11.41 *"at our request a remittance scheme was put into force for the first two parties of technicians, and it was through no fault of ours or indeed of the Ministry's, that it was not a success. The men resented what they felt to be the interference of a local voluntary committee in Jamaica with the paying out of the remittances to their dependants, and they were genuinely confused by the fact that some of their dependants were paying part of their remittances back to the voluntary organisation which had been supporting their dependants before the remittances began to arrive . . . we brought another scheme of remittances for them . . . The difficulties about the remittance schemes remain, and they will not be satisfactorily cleared up until we have the full facts of the working of the scheme in Jamaica from the Governor."*[a]

It seems that under the 'new arrangements' the expatriation allowance which the men only received while they were *"in employment approved by the Department"*, was paid directly to a dependent named by the worker.[b] How the dependents were to survive during periods of unemployment or if the men were not in 'approved' employment did not apparently concern either the Colonial Office or the Ministry. But, given that the men had to go on strike in order to get the expatriation allowance, this is hardly surprising.

There is an internal memorandum indicating that there was some pressure exerted on the men to send extra money to their dependants from their wages.[c] It is also noted that 15 men earning between 75/- and 80/- per week were said to have remitted collectively between £14 and £29 per week to their families. In February 1943 the men on Merseyside were estimated to be collectively sending £100 per week to their relatives.[d] Many men also had savings accounts: the International Labour Organisation Officer reported that 75% of the men in Bolton had such accounts. The average wage earned in Bolton by the men was £9 per week;

[a] CO859/76
[b] LAB26/52
[c] LAB26/52
[d] LAB26/56

exceptionally as much as £17 was earned in a week, at the cost of working well in excess of the average of 70 hours per week.

UNEMPLOYMENT

The West Indians were initially not entitled to receive unemployment benefit as the Assistance Board specifically excluded them: *"it should be noted that a British colonial subject or a British protected person may, for Home Office purposes, be classed as an alien"* and not receive dole. Mr. Keith wrote to J.J. Taylor at the Ministry in February 1942 regarding the West Indians' ineligibility for either sick pay or unemployment benefit and urged that they should be paid a minimum of £2 per week and dependants' allowance. As this was a higher rate than English workers received, Keith explained that such a rate was necessary *"in the case of men who are in lodgings ... they should be able to retain their accommodation as it is difficult for coloured men to get landladies to accept them"*.[a] A protracted struggle with the Assistance Board ensued: at first, the Board wanted to take into consideration the £1 per week expatriation allowance when assessing the right to unemployment benefit. The Colonial Office pointed out that the allowance was being paid directly to dependants in the West Indies. The Board made a new offer: 10/- per week pocket money, 30/- per week board and lodging (based on the charges at West Indies House) and, if a man could prove that he had been sending money home regularly from his wages, then the Board would consider a supplement. In June 1942 a Special Scheme for Assistance to Colonials was drawn up.[b] This provided for colonial workers not resident in Britain before 3.9.38 who were not covered by existing schemes and who were in distress because of sickness or unemployment. Though paragraph 7 of the Circular reiterated that *"British subjects may, for Home Office purposes, be classified as alien"*, assistance could, in future, be paid to *"distressed"* persons. The Board would, however, recover the moneys paid out to Colonials from the Colonial Office Vote. By November 1942 pressure from the Listowel Committee (on the Welfare of Colonial Peoples in the United Kingdom) succeeded in removing para. 7 from the Circular.

[a] CO876/12   [b] Assistance Board Circular (1942) No24 (A24/42)

WHITE ATTITUDES AND PRACTICES TOWARDS WEST INDIAN WORKERS

Throughout the war instances of racialism and the existence of a colour bar were frequently reported: Black workers and soldiers (even Victoria Cross winners) were excluded from restaurants, dance halls, official recreation centres and hotels; The Bishop of Salisbury warned young women against making the acquaintance or taking walks with soldiers of African blood; and though the colour bar in all the armed services was lifted for the duration of the war, newspapers carried stories of British Blacks being refused by the forces and the Women's Land Army.[11]

The *New Statesman and Nation* briefly mentioned the West Indian workers on 6.6.42: *"what should shame us far more deeply is the social colour snobbery with which they are often treated. They live among working people and meet it in its crudest form. People who should know better are equally guilty ... they are refused admittance to dance halls, turned out of hotels, separated from white men in fire watching parties ... people do not know where their own Empire is, nor who inhabits it".*

Learie Constantine spent much of his time addressing local groups, Rotary Clubs, Whitley Councils, etc. on the subject of racial prejudice. But when Arnold Watson wanted to educate a wider public in a BBC talk, the following passages were deleted from his talk: the definition of slaves as *"with no civil status, without the possibility of legal marriage, without rights over their children, incapable of owning real property"*; and *"in the days when there was a boom in unemployment the experiment* (of importing Black workers) *would have been frustrated, since the white man would have felt it was his job that was being taken by a coloured man, and the coloured man might have lost it again because of the colour bar".*[a]

Mr. Keith, the Colonial Office's Senior Welfare Officer, was also dissatisfied with the futility of tackling discrimination on an individual level. Though the memorandum he wrote for his Secretary of State on this subject has not been preserved, his report on the Welfare of Colonial People in the UK, dated 13.11.41

[a] LAB26/53

indicates its contents: "... *suggestions for bringing about an improvement in public opinion on the difficult question of the colour bar in this country. I was also anxious that some positive action should be taken such as legislation to support the common law rights of persons of all races in obtaining refreshment and hospitality in hotels ... I am disappointed that nothing seems to be able to be done in these directions ... I have broached the question of doing something through the schools to improve the teaching about Colonial people and the inculcation of better manners among schoolchildren towards coloured people. My approach has not been very successful. The Board of Education see difficulties in the way of carrying out our wishes. The somewhat negative attitude of some Government Departments towards the colour bar inclines one to think that there is much to be said for a Government statement on the subject.*"[a]

The powerlessness and helplessness of the Colonial Office welfare team was demonstrated by the lack of a government statement and by the escalation of racial discrimination. When the government did eventually make a statement, it was only to condemn, in most general terms, discrimination against Black *British* subjects. After Learie Constantine had brought a private action against the Imperial Hotel for refusing to let him and his family occupy their pre-booked room, questions were asked in the House. Herbert Morrison, the Home Secretary replied: "... *legal proceedings are under way, so I can't express an opinion on the legal aspect. Hotels can only deny accommodation on some reasonable ground, for example that a traveller is not in a fit state to be received. Apart, however, from any question of law, the House will, I am sure, agree with me that there is a responsibility on all members of the community, including not only those who manage hotels and places of public resort but also their clients and guests, to avoid any discrimination against a fellow British subject on the grounds of race or colour. If in this case there has been a failure to accord the full equality of status and treatment to which he is entitled, I would assure him that any such failure is deeply deplored and strongly condemned by responsible public opinion throughout the UK.*"[12]

Some of the evidence for racialism and discrimination at the work place has already been cited. Both were widespread among

[a]CO859/76

government officials, voluntary bodies, management and labour. Take for instance: *"Our contacts with the Ministry of Supply are now close enough to ensure that on the managerial side there is no improper discrimination."*[a] *"Mr Watson has evidently been most successful in understand their (the West Indians) somewhat peculiar mentality."*[13,b] Mr. Caradog Jones, Chairman of the Liverpool Association for the Welfare of Coloured People, writing to the Secretary of State for the Colonies on 11.2.41 hoped that the West Indians would be repatriated at the end of the war. *"The dangers inherent in the importation of coloured workers... could be minimised provided that the men received full equality of economic and social status with their co-workers..."*[c] Even the position of Ernest Bevin, Minister for Labour, was ambiguous: when Vernon Bartlett, MP, asked in the House that the Government should *"discourage the racial discrimination which exists in a number of firms"*, Bevin replied: *"Let me have the facts and I'll deal with them"*. Bartlett answered that *"the facts had been sent to the department"*.[d]

It is hardly surprising that the efforts of neither of the well-meaning welfare staffs made much of an impression on these entrenched attitudes and practices. As indicated, they received no support from their superiors, from other government departments or from ministers of state in their attempts to bring about some change.

Of the attitudes of the local white communities other than that discussed in the section on Housing, the files reveal very little. There is only one file which provides a glimpse, that of the International Labour Organisation report on Bolton. The ILO officer reported that the West Indians told him that *"they are regarded in the towns as an interesting if minor novelty, and that their position would rapidly deteriorate were there many more of them"*. (There were 45, 8 living in lodgings and 37 in a segregated hostel named Colonial House.) The ILO officer commented that the *"West Indians are popular with the local women ... this is not always liked by the male element, and still less by the parents. There does not seem to be really active antagonism"*. The officer wondered if the position of Colonial House on a *"superior"* road in the town might have *"added to the men's*

[a] J.J. Taylor to Creech Jones MP, 1/7/42, in LAB26/52
[b] Memorandum of West Indian Artificers by Major Orde Browne, Special Adviser on Labour to the Colonial Office, 9/10/42 in CO876/46
[c] CO859/75

acceptability".[a]

Though much of Richmond's work needs to be reinterpreted, his data ragarding the relationship of West Indians with white women is similar to that of the ILO. He notes that up to 1944 15% of the craftsmen and 22% of the trainees had married in England; "*the prejudice against the association of Negroes and white girls ... were naturally extended to the idea of intermarriage. In a number of cases girls proposing to marry on the West Indians were evicted by their families and forbidden to come near home again unless they gave up the idea of marrying coloured men. Sometimes the arrival of a baby would be the occasion of some measure of reconciliation, but the father was rarely accepted into the family circle. There were some notable exceptions to this attitude ... such cases seem to have been the exception rather than the rule*".[b]

Teh prevalence and ubiquity of hostility to Black/white relationships is further indicated in a report of Constantine's dated 24.11.41, where he cites an incidence of a policeman in Liverpool who molested a Black worker and his white companion. The two were on their way to the cinema when the policeman stopped them in the street, abused them both and forced to to separate.[c]

The League of Coloured People reported in its November 1942 *Newsletter* the results of their investigations into the conditions under which the men in Liverpool were living: "*practically no social amenities ... local Churches appear to have done nothing to meet their need ... refused the positions in the factories to which they were entitled by their skill ... one man refused communion in Church ...*".

THE END OF THE SCHEME

In their March '43 letter of praise regarding the performance of the trainees, the North-West Training Committee wrote that "*... it is the unanimous view of the Committee that as the men*

[a] CO876/48
[b] Richmond, p83
[c] CO859/76

already brought over had given every satisfaction, it would be desirable to explore the possibility of arrangements being made for further batches of men to be recruited in the West Indies and brought to this country under similar conditions".[a]

Unknown to the Committee, the decision to end the scheme had already been taken. J. Megson, the Colonial Office's Senior Staff Officer, wrote to the Ministry on 16.1.43: *"Although many of the technicians who have been brought over here are successful in employment, grave social problems arise when West Indians are settled in hostels or in camps in this country. The expense is also very great . . . having regard to the present difficult shipping position . . . the recruitment of West Indians personnel for work in this country should in future be restricted."*[b] Arnold Watson expressed his dissatisfaction with this to the Ministry on 2 February 1943: *"we should have been glad to have the further 50 West Indians . . . but it would not, I think, be wise for us to press the Colonial Office if they wish to stop recruiting them . . . I am personally sorry that the experiment should stop here."* Leopold replied from the Ministry's HQ on 20 February 1943 *"I feel some regret that we cannot continue this experiment . . ."* The Colonial Office confirmed the cessation of recruitment on February 22nd in their letter to the Ministry: *"As regards resumption of recruitment . . . owing to the shortage of shipping and other difficulties, recruitment of West Indians for work in this country should in future be restricted to certain classes of skilled workers, and then only considered in individual cases in which openings for employment here are known to exist."*

Why, the *"experiment"* having proved a success, were more workers from the Caribbean not brought to Britain? What were these *"shipping and other difficulties"*? And why were skilled men only to be accepted as individuals and not in groups? The answers lie, I think, in a change of circumstances in the Caribbean playing into the Colonial Office's hands, and in the attitude of the men in power in the Colonial Office towards the presence of Black 'colonials' in Britain.

Harold Macmillan, appointed Under Secretary of State for the Colonies in January 1942, revived the Colonial Office's struggle to convince the War Office that they should employ West Indians in pioneer units for overseas service. The issue was discussed at a

[a] LAB19/97   [b] CO323/1863, file 9351/1B

meeting in Mr. Macmillan's rooms on April 14 and the Ministry with the War Office. Brigadier Piggott, the War Office's representative, was disinclined to accept a West Indian Pioneer Unit for overseas service. He suggested *"there was plenty of work in this country on which military labour could be deployed"*. Mr Macmillan pressed for overseas service: though the previous Egyptian Government had refused to have West Indian Pioneer Units on its soil, he pointed out that *"it was possible that the new Government would not wish to maintain this objection"*. (As Egypt was a British protectorate at this time, its Government was in no position to make such pronouncements. According to a memo dated 13 December 1941[a] it was the Commander-in-Chief, Middle East, who turned down the offer of West Indian labour.) Furthermore, as the Commander-in-Chief, Middle East, had cabled the Governor of the Seychelles direct asking for pioneer units for the Middle East, there was an obvious need for labour corps. Mr. Macmillan also referred to the *"anomalous situation which now exists by reason of the fact that whereas no opportunity is given to West Indians to enlist in the British Army, West Indians can and do enlist in substantial numbers in the Canadian Forces in Canada and are now serving with such forces in this country"*.[b] The Ministry of Labour was in favour of West Indians being recruited into pioneer corps to work in Britain, but only if certain conditions were met. Mr. Bevin had given very clear instructions to his representative at the meeting: *"I cannot see why this type of labour should be specially selected not to receive British wages. When the skilled men were brought to this country they were treated as Britishers, and why unskilled labour* (in pioneer units) *should be selected for special treatment I cannot understand. I should not object to the War Office organising a Pioneer Corps in the West Indies on British rates of pay and allowances, and they could then, as they do with their own Pioneer Corps, lend units out to agriculture or for such work as drainage... but it is essential that they should be treated in exactly the same way as our own Corps. ... On the wider issue, I am very much concerned at any suggestion that coloured people should receive differential treatment. It savours so much of the 19th century. ... The second point is that the Americans are using this labour at fairly good rates of pay, I understand, on the work at their bases in British Colonies. What is likely to be the reaction,*

[a] CO968/38/1   [b] LAB13/37

therefore, to any proposal for recruiting them into a Pioneer Corps, at military rates of pay, solely for the purpose of their doing work ordinarily performed by civilians? Will it not appear as a subterfuge to obtain cheap labour? . . .". The decision reached was to ask the Secretary of State for War to approve "*the raising of units in principle*". The Executive Committee of the Army Council acknowledged the request in a letter to the Ministry dated May 31, which stated that there was "*no objection in principle to the employment of West Indian Pioneer Corps in the UK, but the shipping position forbade such employment as a practical issue*".[a]

It is difficult to understand why there was suddenly a problem over shipping as at the April meeting it was concluded that "*the shipping difficulty did not arise*". There was further confirmation of this on 22 November 1942 in a telegram from the Washington Embassy stating that shipping was available.[b] Thus the conflict between the Colonial Office, who had to solve their colonial dilemma, and the War Office, who clearly had no intention at this stage of the war of using West Indians, continued.

Mr. Bevin had seen the position clearly. If they could obtain work locally, men from the Caribbean saw no reason for going to Britain except in the uniforms of the armed services to gain honour and glory as combatant troops. John Keith of the Colonial Office admitted to Arnold Watson in a letter dated 27 January 1943, "*the position is that in answer to the appeal for 200* (unskilled men for GTC training), *only 145 came forward*".[c] As already stated, during 1941/42, the boom years of employment on the US bases in the Caribbean, there was full employment throughout the British West Indian islands except in Jamaica. This happy situation continued for the war years in Trinidad which housed the largest US base, and in British Guina where rice and bauxite production were almost doubled.[14] Workers much preferred to travel inter-island than to sail to distant Britain where wages were low, taxes high and the weather inclement. So many skilled workers had left Barbados by 1942 that on March 7 the Barbados Government issued a proclamation forbidding foundry workers, turners, machinists, fitters, moulders and welders from leaving the island.[15] Trinidad experienced a net in-migration of 21,799 during the war.[16]

[a] LAB13/37 [c] LAB18/97
[b] CO968/74/18

Unemployment in Jamaica was only slightly relieved by employment on the US base. However, as American recruitment of labour for the Panama Canal Zone recommenced in 1941 and rumours circulated that 10,000 or more would be needed, it is hardly surprising that very few answered the Overseas Volunteers Committee's advertisement of June 6, 1941 for labour for the UK. The Committee re-advertised on June 11, *"urging mechanics to answer the appeal for skilled workers.... The Committee feel that there are many competent mechanics in the country and parishes and to these a special appeal is being made. With the sugar crop having been reaped, there are several mechanics formerly employed on sugar estates who should prove suitable...."*[17]. But even this did not influence the Jamaicans, who either hoped for work in Panama or the more lucrative jobs on the base, where the pay scale began at 10d. per hour for a 48-hour week, plus free accommodation, free medical services, subsidised meals and almost unlimited overtime.

By 1942, when the base was laying off workers, the Jamaicans must have realised that with the US entry into the war, their labour would be needed again in the USA, and they would be able to earn far more than the 65/6 (less tax) being offered to GTC trainees in the UK. Moreover, working in the US meant being away from home for only six months at a time, while the British contracts were for the duration of the war. Judging by the numbers who eventually went to the USA as contract workers, Jamaicans much preferred to work for high wages for short periods close to home and in a country with which many of them were familiar.

REPATRIATION

As stated earlier, the Colonial Office was always in favour of repatriating men they considered *"centres of discontent and ill feeling"*.[a] But the men refused to be repatriated. In order to avoid the police issuing the repatriation notices, some moved from their

[a] Orde Browne Report CO876/46

lodgings and took new jobs; some joined the Merchant Navy. A few, probably not more than 10, including some men who were ill, accepted repatriation in 1943.

His Majesty's Government had to find a way of regaining control of rebellious Black workers. In May 1943, perhaps as a result of Dr. Blacklock's complaints to the Secretary of State, or because the Ministry of Supply wanted to discharge 130 men on the grounds of *"serious misconduct"* (but could not do so under the special employment conditions prevailing during wartime), the Colonial Office evolved a new tactic. It was decided that the Defence Regulations should be changed so as to include Colonials resident in the UK in the call-up for the armed forces. Accordingly, an Order in Council was passed in mid-1943, *"enabling West Indian men in the UK not giving good performance to be called up"* for military service.[a] In December 1943, seven men received call-up papers, but had worked out how to circumvent the Government's dictum to fight or go home: six joined the Merchant Navy, and one found a job to his liking in an 'approved' factory. We do not know if any of the West Indians were called up under the powers of this Order; all the files reveal is that 28 craftsmen joined the Merchant Navy and two H.M. Forces.[18] However, as the Ministry of Labour circular 120/9 of February 1944 specifically excluded Colonial technicians and trainees from call-up, it is most likely that HMG gave up this particular attempt to control Black workers.

Though the scheme was ended in 1943, the men already here were kept in employment until almost the end of the war. It was not until early 1945 that letters were sent to the men asking who wanted early repatriation. Apparently only 35 replied affirmatively, and this caused some consternation at the Ministry. *"It would be undesirable to encourage them to remain in this country . . . we simply cannot face the consequences of having redundant West Indians hanging about in the N-W unemployed"*, Miss Barbara Green of the Ministry's Welfare Department replied to Learie Constantine when he wrote suggesting that probably only 50% of the men would wish to go home. Miss Green did not state why skilled West Indians would necessarily and inevitably *"hang around the N-W unemployed"*, or why the consequences of Blacks being unemployed were more fearful than white unemployment.[19,b]

[a] CO876/47   [b] LAB26/134

87

The men themselves wrote to both Constantine and the Secretary of State for the Colonies, expressing their apprehensions about going home: *"we are only going home to swell the ranks of the unemployed. . . . All we want is assurance of employment when we get home. . . . Remember we have no unemployment benefit and old age pensions or dole at home. . . . Quite a lot of promises have been made to us but none fulfill* (sic)*. . . . We feel we should be sent to a job or if possible priority should be given us. . . ."*.[a] Two men even wrote to Jamaica's Governor: *"we answered the call for Munitions Workers to work in the UK at a time when our dear Mother Country needed all the help she could get. . . . We thought it our solemn duty to do what we could, small as it may be, to help rid the world of Nazism . . ."*, and asked that their contracting/building business, which they hoped to resuscitate on their return, should be given some preference. The only response they received were forms to fill in for the Re-absorption Committee.[20]

The men's fears were well-founded. The 1945-46 report on *Development and Welfare in the West Indies* admitted that *"towards the end of 1945 unemployment in Jamaica and Barbados threatened to become acute, mainly because of large-scale repatriation of workers from employment in the United States and to a lesser degree the return of demobilised service men . . . "*.[21] It is therefore not surprising that assurances of jobs were not forthcoming and that very little was done in the West Indies to resettle returning workers; some men even found their old employers reneging on promises to re-employ them on their return. The *Colonial Report for Jamaica for 1946* admitted that there were problems with resettling ex-servicemen; there was a shortage of building materials preventing the construction of promised new housing; funds were not available for land settlement, business loans or technical training. The Mother Country did not deem it necessary to allocate funds to her West Indian colonies to help resettle those women and men who had made sacrifices to ensure her victory in her hour of need.

In the North-West, by the end of the year many West Indians were unemployed or having to contend with their workmates asking them when they were going home. On November 17 the Colonial Office's representative in Liverpool reported that *"it is*

[a] LAB26/134

agreed that there is a growing tendency for employers to seek English labour rather than accept Colonials sent to them".[a] In October 1946 32 of the men were registered as unemployed on Merseyside.

The men who had accepted repatriation fared no better. The 34 men, seven wives and seven children who were supposed to sail in September were still waiting in port at the beginning of November because returning Canadians were being given priority. On November 7 a further 18 men, four wives and five children joined those already waiting.

By the end of November the situation of these men and their families was so desperate that Learie Constantine threatened to resign if nothing were done to expedite matters. Despite this protest, it was not until December 10th that berths were found — and then only for the men. When space was found for the families, for whom the Ministry only agreed to pay fares after lengthy discussions with the Colonial Office, we do not know.

The question of post-war training in Britain was raised as early as August 1943 by some of the workers in Bolton who wrote to David Adams MP, asking for training, the possibility of emigration to other British colonies as there was no industry in the West Indies, or work on post-war projects.[b] The men were keen to better themselves: despite the long hours they worked the Bolton men attended classes or took correspondence courses in subjects as diverse as welding, chartered accountancy and electrical engineering. The question of offering post-war training to the men was not raised until the Conference on the Disposal of Colonial War Workers held in October 1944, when it was suggested that both colonial servicemen and workers should be eligible for training.[c] The Ministry of Education acceded to the request and the workers were informed in November 1945 that they would be eligible for the Further Education and Vocational Training Scheme. The men had to apply to the Colonial Office for permission to apply to the Scheme; by February 1946, 153 had received approval and 17 were rejected. **Those approved had to agree to return to their colonies on completion of their courses.** Eight months later, in October 1946, 96 men were still waiting for a decision from the Ministry of Education regarding their applications for courses.

[a] LAB26/134
[b] CO876/48
[c] CO876/44

According to Richmond only *"about twelve men received grants"* thus throwing considerable doubt on the Ministry's good faith.[a]

It is impossible to establish from the remaining files what happend to either the men who stayed or those who returned home. 102 men accepted repatriation; Richmond quotes from letters detailing the hardship and unemployment the men faced in the West Indies (pp.141-2).[22,b] Constantine had also received letters claiming that those *"who had been rapatriated* (to Jamaica) *found on arrival that there was nothing done for them"*; the letters, said Constantine, expressed considerable cynicism.[c] Of those who remained, at the moment we know nothing. The files' only comment is that three men had opened shops in Liverpool.

By March 1947 some of the men were back in England, seeking employment and combatting an even more aggressive racism by the community, the workers, the unions, the employers and government. Today, some 35 years later, these racist forces persist.

[a] Richmond, p135
[b] Richmond, pp141-2
[c] LAB26/134

Notes and References

INTRODUCTION

1 Reported in the West India Committee Circular, 17/10/1940.
2 West India Royal Commission Report, HMSO, 1945 (usually known as the Moyne Commission).

    The papers of the Advisory Committee on the Welfare of Colonial People in the United Kingdom were loaned to me by a member of that Committee.

MAIN TEXT

1 For instance, before the war, only 5% of the arable land in Barbados was used for growing food.
2 W D Rasmussen: *A history of the emergency farm labour supply program 1943-47*, Agriculture Monograph No 13, Washington, 1951.
3 Hansard 23/3/42, vol 378, col 2005 and 15/7/43, vol 391, cols 392-3.
4 M E Fletcher: *Report on an Investigation into the Colour Problem in Liverpool and other Ports*, Liverpool Assoc. for the Welfare of Half-caste Children, Liverpool 1930.
5 M Caradog Jones: *The Economic Status of Coloured Families in the Port of Liverpool*, University Press of Liverpool, 1940.
6 M Caradog Jones: *Survey of Merseyside*, University Press of Liverpool, 1940.
7 Learie Constantine, MBE: *Colour Bar*, London, 1954, p.136.
8 A H Richmond: *Colour Prejudice in Britain*, London, 1954, pp71-77.
9 Hansard 18/11/42, vol 385, cols 348-9.
10 A. Watson: *West Indian Workers in Britain*, London, 1942.
11 *Daily Herald* 22/9/42.
12 Hansard 23/9/43, vol 392, cols 443-4.
13 G. St. J. Orde Browne held all the Victorian attitudes towards Blacks. While Head of the Labour Department in Tanganyika he wrote: "*tribesmen tended to become thriftless and improvident ... he lived mainly for the moment, expecting the leaders of the community to make such arrangements as they might consider advisable, and relying confidently on the success of concerted effort to meet calamity.... Being largely relieved of the results of his own foolishness or incompetence by the generous aid of his neighbour...* (p. 19) ... *In government he seems to be distinctly lacking in capacity when entirely free from European control or advice...*" (p. 11) (from Orde Browne: *The African Labourer*, OUP, 1933).
14 Sir F Stockdale: *Development and Welfare in the West Indies, 1943-44*, HMSO, Colonial No 189, 1945.
15 Barbados *Observer*, March 7 1942.
16 R Kuczynski: *A Demographic Survey of the British Colonial Empire*, Vol III, OUP, 1953.
17 *The Gleaner* (Jamaica) June 6 and June 11, 1941.

18 Richmond gives a total of 34 men as having joined the Merchant Navy or HM Forces (p. 134).
19 The number of men registered as unemployed in Liverpool in April 1945 was 3156. By November this had risen to 10,751 and by April 1946 to 22,665 (*Ministry of Labour Gazette*). For an analysis of Liverpool's history of unemployment since its heyday as a slave-trading port, see Merseyside Socialist Research Group: *Merseyside in Crisis*, 23 Glover St, Birkenhead, 1980.
20 Barbados Archives, CSO 1141/42/S13.
21 Sir J. MacPherson: *Development and Welfare in the West Indies, 1945-46*, HMSO, 1947.
22 One worker on his way home ended up in a mental hospital in Florida. The psychiatric report stated that he was suffering from "*mild or early paranoia... condition probably aggravated by the tensions under which he has been working in England...*" (file no. 1600/42, found in the basement of Headquarters House, Kingston, Jamaica).

3. The British Honduran Forestry Unit in Scotland 1941-43

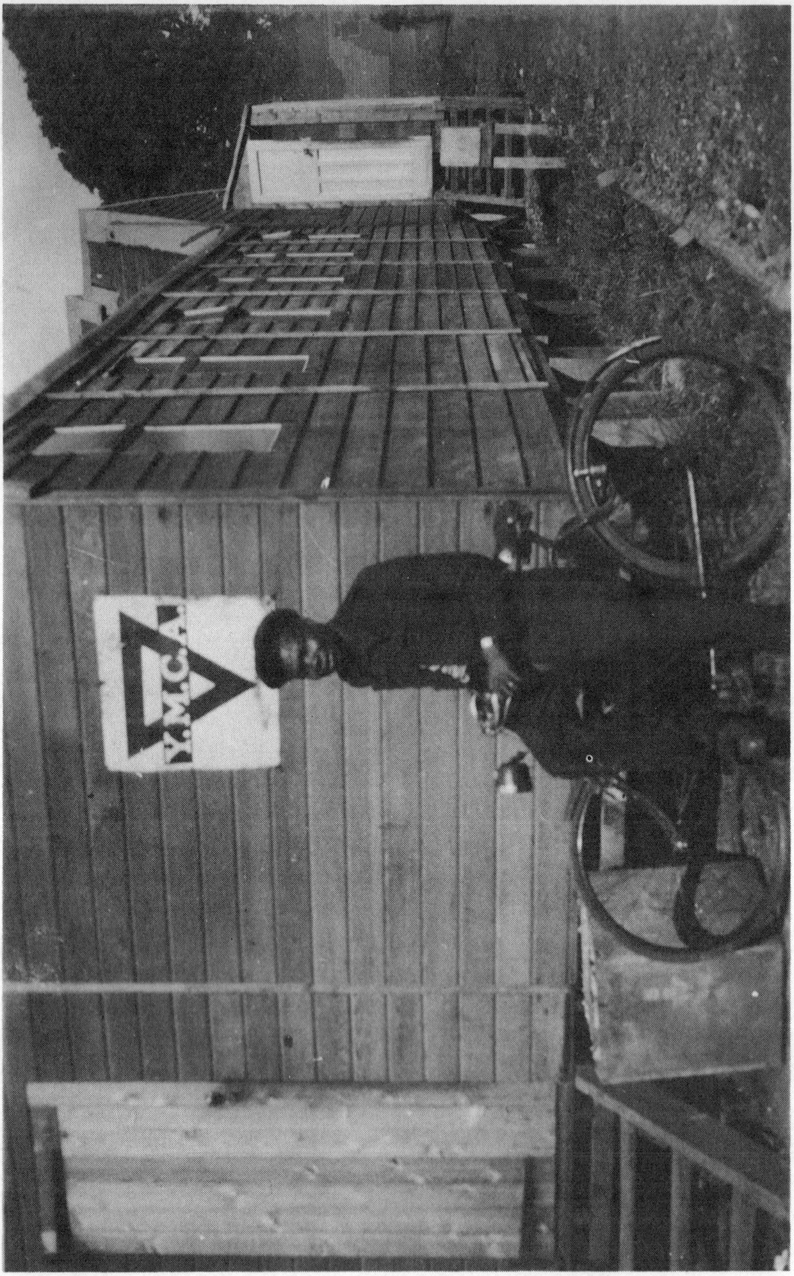
YMCA

i. **INTRODUCTION**

The two essential ingredients to the successful conduct of a non-nuclear war are manpower and materials. Timber is one of these essential materials.

By 1939, as 95% of Britain's timber requirements were met by imports, the industry had contracted to 15,000 workers. Soon after the outbreak of war, Britain's timber suppliers fell into enemy hands and the shipments of timber from free Canada ceased because of the devastations wrought by German submarines. This situation placed Britain in a dilemma: home-grown timber supplies had to be increased, whilst there was little labour to achieve this. The Forestry Commission eked out its labour force with women, schoolboys on holidays, conscientious objectors and resident refugee aliens. Highly-skilled timber workers were put on the Schedule of Reserved Occuptions to ensure that they would not be called up. At the end of the year, 2,000 loggers were imported from Newfoundland. In 1940, six military forestry units from Australia and New Zealand arrived. In 1941 the Forestry Commission was incorporated with the Ministry of Supply and renamed the Home-Grown Timber Department; 20 Canadian military forestry units were added to the Home-Grown Timber Department's labour force. At the end of the year, 539 civilian loggers arrived from British Honduras. In 1942, the newly set up Women's Timber Corps, another ten Canadian units, 339 British Hondurans, at least 3,000 Italian prisoners of war and imported Irish labour swelled the ranks of forestry workers to a peak of 73,000 in June, 1943. Yet in September, 1943 it was decided, specifically and perversely, that "there was no longer any necessity to retain the (British Hondurans) in this country".[1]

This essay will attempt to examine why, at a time of great labour shortage, it was decided to dismiss the British Honduran Forestry Unit only some eleven months after the second contingent had arrived in Britain. The argument advanced by the historian of the Home-Grown Timber Department, R. Meiggs, that as the Battle of the Atlantic was virtually over shipping could recommence and that in any case standing timber in the UK was seriously depleted, is an insufficient argument for dismissal and repatriation, especially when Meiggs states a little further on in his account that by 1943 there was an urgent need for foresters around the Mediterranean, in Western Europe and in New Guinea. Most of the military forestry companies in Britain were, in fact, despatched to these areas. Furthermore, as Meiggs also states, since during 1944-45 the Home-Grown Timber Department replaced 'unsuitable' Italian prisoners of war with 4,000 German prisoners, obviously timber production continued in Britain.

In order to discover the reasons for the British Honduran Forestry Unit's dismissal, I have examined the few government records which have been retained at the Public Records Office. Unfortunately, most have been destroyed, as have all the relevant Scottish records. This meagre information has been supplemented by correspondence and interviews with some of the officials still alive and some of the residents from villages which were near the Hondurans' camps.

ii. BRITISH HONDURAS (BELIZE)

Background Information

British Honduras (Belize), in the 1940s the only British colony in Central America, stretches 174 miles from Mexico in the north to Guatemala in the south. Guatemala also borders it to the west; the distance from the sea to the western border never exceeds 70 miles. The coastline is swampy; the southern half of the country is mountainous; extensive river systems drain both the northern and southern plains. The climate is tropical; hurricanes have occasionally devastated coastal towns and plantations.

Chicle and mahogany were until recently British Honduras' main exports. Chicle was tapped from the sapodilla tree and exported to the US where, before the post-war advent of synthetic substitutes, it formed the main ingredient of chewing-gum. Mahogany used to be cut in the Gallon Jug area, rafted down river to Belize City and shipped from there to the furniture manufacturers in the US and Europe. Bananas used to be grown for export in the Stann Creek valley until 1917 when Panama disease became a serious problem. Citrus fruit exported as juice and concentrate replaced bananas as an export crop. The production of sugar, grown in the north, seldom exceeded local demand.

History

The Mayas, whose empire encompassed the area now known as Belize, migrated northwards some hundreds of years before Spaniards first sailed along the coast in 1506. The first Europeans in the area came not as settlers but as pirates and buccaneers, who found convenient hiding-places for their ships behind the treacherous waters created by the reefs and cays along the coast. By the first half of the 17th century, when the price of logwood (used for dyes in the English woollen industry) rose to £100 per ton, some English buccaneers decided to settle in order to join in this lucrative trade by exploiting the local forests. They were soon joined by settlers from Jamaica, both English and Spanish, equally eager to get rich quickly.

As the treaties between England and Spain never defined the position of the English logwood cutters on the Spanish Main, the Spaniards attacked them periodically. The attacks ceased after the settlers, with help from the British in Jamaica, soundly defeated the Spanish in 1798. The political status of the area was not settled until 1862 when it officially became a British colony. Within nine years of achieving this status, the government of British Honduras was changed from an elected assembly to a nominated council with all power concentrated in the hands of the Governor. In 1935, an elected element, with the franchise based on property qualification, was introduced. Of the 1,156 eligible to vote in the 1939 elections, only 789 went to the ballot-box.

British colonial policy has always been the maximisation of profits from exploitation of the natural and other resources of the colonies. Thus in British Honduras a few large expatriate companies were granted vast tracts of land for the exploitation of forest products, especially chicle and mahogany (logwood declined in importance by the 19th century). By the 1960s, 35% of the total area was in the hands of 50 people, of whom 47 were absentee landlords. The government owned 60% of the land — largely the mountain areas; ½% of the land was under cultivation. The companies incurred almost no costs: wages were extremely low;

outlay for capital equipment almost nil; taxation was minimal and re-afforestation not required.

Population

British Honduras might well have a greater mixture of peoples than the remainder of the Caribbean. To the English and Spanish settlers the following peoples have been added:

> free blacks and 'coloureds';
>
> several thousand black Caribs (the offspring of Caribs and slaves) deported after an unsuccessful rebellion against the British in 1795;
>
> Chinese and Indian workers imported as indentured labour for the sugar plantations;
>
> Spanish and mestizo refugees fleeing from Mexico;
>
> returning Mayas.

Social and Economic Conditions

In the words of the Senior Medical Officer, British Honduras was *"a very backward colony"*. In 1938, there were only 35 miles of all-weather roads and 25 miles of railway; the 7 hospitals which all *"require[d] a considerable amount of modernising"* provided a total of 66 beds and a staff of 17 nurses. The infant mortality rate was 12.91% (the highest in the British West Indies), the maternal mortality rate was two and a half times that in England. Though nutritional diseases were not common, malaria was; VD was *"very prevalent and treatment little sought for"*. 10,431 pupils, that is, approximately two thirds of the school-age population, were enrolled in 79 schools, of which only five were secondary; the pupil/teacher ratio was 63:1. The largest single item of expenditure in the annual budget was for the police.

Industrial development was very limited: there were six small factories: two making cigarettes, one each making soap, starch, citrus juice and cohane oil, there was a small sugar mill/factory near Corozal. The timber industry, which accounted for 75.7% of exports in 1937, only acquired its first modern sawmill in 1933; by 1937, 50% of the timber exported was still unmanufactured wood, mainly mahogany. The introduction of tractors for timber haulage was relatively recent.

There were no trade unions, no workers' compensation schemes and no fixed minimum wage: un- and under-employment were chronic. Wages were low: a carpenter in government employment was paid a maximum of 45 pence per day; mahogany loggers working in isolated camps for only six months of the year earned between £2.50 and £3.50 per month, plus rations. In contrast, the Governor's salary was almost £2,000 per annum, and even the lowest grade agricultural officer earned £370 p.a.

iii. RECRUITMENT

British Honduras

In 1939, the newly-appointed Labour Officer to the Government of British Honduras met a situation described by the Governor in a telegram to the Colonial Office on March 13th, 1939 as *". . . suffering and uneasiness acute in Belize. Due to unemployment. Developing into a dangerous situation"*. The position had not improved by the middle of July, 1940, when the Labour Officer's memorandum to the Colonial Office read: *"Our immediate problem is unemployment with attendant starvation and social unrest. Things here are bad, very bad"*. Not surprisingly, therefore, when the Colonial Office telegrammed the Governor on May 23rd, 1941 asked if up to 500 foresters could be made available for work in Britain, the immediate reply was *"no problem"*.

The Colonial Office, negotiating on behalf of the Ministry of Supply to whom they had proposed the use of British Honduran Foresters, informed the Govenor of the Ministry's requirements in terms of the crafts and skills required. The Governor replied with a warning: *"this is logging country, not lumbering"*; the required number of sawyers was *"impossible. . . even six will strain our resources"*; he also pointed out that even in Panama the men had earned better wages. However, as the requirement for imported labour in Central America had diminished drastically at the outbreak of war, despite the low wages being offered when recruitment began in July, 1938 men applied. Of these, 857 were rejected on medical grounds; the 541 men accepted left Belize on August 5th, 1941.

The contract which the men signed provided for:
1. free transport to and from the forestry camps in Britain;
2. a working week of 48 hours for a wage of £3 less board and lodging;
3. free medical services;
4. tools and an initial supply of working clothes and boots (replacements had to be paid for);
5. a term of engagement of three years or the durations of the war, whichever the less;
6. termination of employment by one month's notice by the Officer-in-Charge;
7. unsatisfactory work or conduct punishable by instant dismissal and repatriation;
8. bad or indifferent work or misbehaviour punishable by a fine or reduction in pay;
9. half-pay for days lost due to illness; no pay for days lost due to bad weather (however, if a man's work was satisfactory, in bad weather he had to be paid a minimum of 75 pence a week;
10. incapacitated men come under the provisions of the UK Workmen's Compensation Act, but were liable to dismissal and repatriation if unable to work;
11. transfer to any other employment or to the armed forces was forbidden;
12. immediate return to British Honduras on the expiration of the contract (though special permission to remain in the UK temporarily for a specified period could be sought from the Officer-in-Charge).

This was effectively indentured labour.

Britain

The Governor's enthusiasm for getting rid of part of his unemployed labor force, even if it meant losing some of the Colony's skilled workers, was not matched by those awaiting the men's arrival in

Britain. Mr Robinson, Chairman of the Forestry Commission, "*was not in favour at any stage at* (sic) *bringing over coloured labour which he thought* (would be) *unworkable in this country*". The Duke of Buccleuch, a large landowner in southwest Scotland, whose timber was to be cut for war purposes, was remembered by J. L. Keith, Senior Welfare Officer at the Colonial Office, as raising "*a lot of objections when it was proposed to bring the British Honduran foresters over*... (he) *thought a good deal of police control would be required*". Sir S. Strong Steel, Director of the Home-Grown Timber Department, in a memorandum dated July 3rd 1941, did not "*feel inclined to take responsibility for placing these men from British Honduras on private estates close to houses and cottages occupied by estate employees*".

Scotland

Scotland during the war was teeming with foreigners. Most of the 40,000 Polish troops in Britain by 1941 were in camps in Scotland, as were the Free French Army; there were Polish, French and Norwegian naval units on Clydeside. Belgian, Dutch, Czech, Polish and Norwegian civilians were settled there and Spanish Republican and other European pioneer corps were sent to work throughout the area. By June 1944 almost a million US Army troops, of whom approximately 10% were Blacks, had disembarked at the Clyde docks. The English evacuees, war-workers, troops and RAF were also regarded as foreigners by the hard-pressed Scots, most of whose able-bodied men were overseas serving in the armed forces.

The precedent for importing civilian forestry units had been set during World War I, when Newfoundlanders were brought to Britain. It was now again to Newfoundland that the Ministry of Supply first turned: by 1940, 2,000 'Newfie' loggers were working in Scotand. The men were employed on six-monthly contracts at the end of which they could apply for a free passage home, enlist in the British Forces, or re-engage for a further six months. At the end of the first six months, a third of the Newfoundlanders applied to return home, claiming that they had "*received inadequate treatment at the hands of this country*". More men were recruited, on new contracts which were for the duration of the war, thus keeping the strength of the Unit at just over 2,000 men. Conditions, however, did not improve, as Mr Pearson, a representative of the of Health complained of the unsanitary conditions in some of the Newfoundland camps in February, 1942 found them to be *"little more than prisoners' compounds"* with the men *"in almost mutinous condition"*. *"The attitude of the Ministry of Supply seems to be one of indifference...welfare organisation, in so far as it does exist in the Newfoundland Forestry Unit is pitifully inadequate... The Home-Grown Timber Department either do not know or do not care to learn the real conditions under which the men live"*, the officials reported. The Ministry of Supply, forced into investigating the camp conditions by a veritable barrage of letters from Clement Attlee, who besides being Secretary of State for the Dominions was also Deputy Prime Minister, wrote in its report in June, 1942; *"the Unit, having got a bad name at the beginning of its career, has been treated by the Home-Grown Timber Department was annoyance and suspicion, a point of view which was fully appreciated by the Unit... they had been given timber to cut which was situated on very difficult ground and which had been refused by other Units."* This did not bode well for the Hondurans.

The other units referred to by the Ministry were forestry units from the military Companies of Engineers from Australia, Canada and New Zealand: a total number of 6,160 men by July, 1942. As part of the military, these men, and especially the Canadians, came equipped with the most modern machinery and even introduced new techniques of sawmilling. The Canadians who had come as self-contained units (whereas the Australians and New Zealanders needed unskilled workers for such work as clearing, burning, stacking and loading), showed the highest production output[2].

As military units these lumbermen had access to Navy, Army & Air Force Institute stores and special places of entertainment reserved for the armed forces, which of course were 'off limits' to the Hondurans and Newfoundlanders.

iv. ARRIVAL

The First Contingent

Because of wartime shipping difficulties the Hondurans had a very complicated journey to Britain via Trinidad and Halifax: 267 men arrived in Liverpool in August on the S.S.Orbita and a further 114 early in September on the S.S.Strathaird. The remainder of the men were delayed in Trinidad, missed their troopship convoy in Halifax, and were eventually torpedoed. Luckily their ship, the S.S.Svend Foyn, managed to limp into Reykjavik harbour without luggage. They finally reached Scotland towards the end of October, 1941. Thus, instead of a summer arrival which would have allowed some time for acclimatisation, the men arrived in the autumn and had to contend with a winter of considerable severity.

The Ministries of Supply and Labour agreed between them that Supply's provisions for the reception, housing and recreational facilities of the Hondurans was adequate. Dr Patterson, the white Medical Officer accompanying the men from Belize, was expected to act as their welfare officer. The Colonial Office, doubting the experience of the other Ministries in dealing with specially imported colonial workers, offered to assist at least in the men's reception. The offer was turned down.

Although the Unit included one foreman, one medical officer, one medical orderly and one officer-in-charge, the men were split into three camps, at Duns and East Linton in southeast Scotland, and Kirkpatrick Fleming some 100 miles away in the south-west. Thus, from the very beginning, it was inevitable that with a numerically inadequate medical/welfare and management team, there would be serious problems. However, it was not this, but the conditions of the camps which worried the officials in the Colonial Office when they visited the camps in mid-September. Their memorandum listed uncompleted heating and hot water services, unlined and too few sleeping huts, unfurnished recreation huts, and not enough lighting (there was no electricity). No warm underwear had been issued and the men were only provided with one suit of working clothes which meant they would have to work in damp clothing as there were no facilities for drying rain-soaked or washed clothes.

The Second Contingent

Despite the dissatisfaction it was constantly expressing about the Hondurans, the Ministry of Supply requested a further 500 men early in 1942. However, as Panama was again recruiting workers, the Governor could not supply the required number: the 331 men engaged arrived in November, 1942 and were sent to camps in Sutherlandshire and Ross-shire in the north of Scotland. The men's winter arrival was mitigated slightly by the northern camps being better laid out and the sleeping huts being of more solid construction. However, all but one of the camps were in extremely isolated areas with no public transport to the nearest towns. Two of the camps were in Protected Areas, which meant that visitors were not allowed. Because of the camps' isolation the YMCA could not undertake to run canteens; these were eventually run in a somewhat haphazard fashion by the Ministry itself. It was ome before any arrangements for leave

ually run in a somewhat haphazard fashion by the Ministry itself. It was some before any arrangements for leave were made: at the end of June, 1943 (i.e. 7 months after arrival), the Colonial Office noted that the men had not yet been on leave and that further welfare measures would need to be taken before the onset of the next winter.

v.   LIFE IN THE CAMPS

These inauspicious beginnings were not followed by rapid improvements. The welfare section of the Colonial Office grew so distressed at what they saw as the inadequacies of the Ministry of Supply that during 1943 they even contemplated suggesting that the Colonial Office should take over the running of the camps.

Clothing

By the end of 1941, after considerable pressure from the Colonial Office, warm underwear was made available but as it had to be paid for, many men refused to buy any. The Colonial Office also found that the second suit of working clothes had not been issued; the boots given to the men were not waterproof, and no gloves had been issued; the huts, especially at East Lindon, were still very cold, and despite the men evidently suffering from the effects of the cold, hot drinks or warm food were not available at midday. The men who had lost all their belongings in the torpedoed ship had received neither compensation nor replacement clothing. (It was not until May, 1942 that compensation was agreed.)

Food

There were also problems over food: the Unit had brought its own cooks, but their expertise with tropical food was inappropriate to the foodstuffs available in war-time Scotland. Added problems were caused by the men being used to a high intake of sugar, which was in very short supply in Britian, and their reluctance to eat mutton or lamb, the most easily obtained meats, but ones with which they were quite unfamiliar. Eventually, at the insistence of Mr Robertson, the Unit's manager, the army sent over some cooks to instruct the Hondurans in the preparation of dried eggs and other war-time delights.

Medical Care

As some of the men had arrived ill and with incompletely treated VD, doubts were cast on the efficiency of Dr Patterson, the Medical Officer who had travelled with the men from Belize. Another doctor was called in to examine the men: fourteen were admitted to hospital, thirty were found to have serious dental problems and twenty-five were suffering from VD. Mr I. Cummings, a Colonial Office Welfare Officer, reported that Dr Patterson, who was also supposed to act as Welfare Officer, was very unpopular with the men and that he spent at least half his time in the comfort of the Unit's headquarters in Edinburgh, the men were receiving inadequate medical attention. Rudolph Dunbar's January 1942 *Report on Social Welfare Among Coloured People on the Tyneside* included an account of the unsatisfactory conditions in the Scottish camps and remarked that the Medical Officer treated everything with pink pills and was very harsh towards the men. Mr Keith, the Colonial Office's Senior Welfare Officer, recommended that Dr Patterson should be sent back to Honduras as he was *"patently unable to carry out the necessary health and welfare measures"*. The Ministry of Supply agreed to this in May, 1942, but it was not until September that Dr Patterson left for Belize. The medical care of the men was then put in the hands of the grossly overworked local GPs, who had to threaten to withdraw their services in order to obtain adequate renumeration from the Ministry of Health.

Health

A survey in July, 1942 found that there had been 32 cases of pulmonary disease, 118 cases of diseases of the digestive system, 83 injuries, 137 *"other ailments"*, 267 *"minor complaints"* and 62 cases of VD. The returns for the quarter ended December 31st, 1942 showed 2389 days lost through illness; for the quarter ended June 30th, 1943, 2909 days had been lost in the southern camps and 1917 in the northern. It has not been possible to compare this with either the incidence of illness or the days lost through illness by other forestry units, though the figures of 28 repatriated on medical grounds compares well with the 144 Newfoundlanders returned home as sick. Nevertheless, the numbers reporting ill, obviously worried the Colonial Office sufficiently for them to suggest (but not until August, 1943, at the time of the repatriation discussions) that *"more effective medical arrangements were necessary and that a Medical Officer should be appointed to the Unit."*

An inordinate amount of attention was paid by the Ministry to the incidence of venereal disease among the men. A special report devoted to VD, dated July 14th, 1943, enumerated in great detail the numbers who had ever suffered from VD and compared these (very unfavourably) with the numbers of VD patients amongst the general population and the army. The report did not examine the incidence of VD in British Honduras where it is endemic. A special section of the Ministry's 1944 Report on the British Honduran Forestry Unit speaks of VD in *"alarming figures"* and states that *"the problem of the prevention of VD in a Unit consisting of coloured men divorced from their families is insoluble... the men were infected when on leave... the provision of prophylactic measures in the camps themselves would be of no use"*. Whether the Ministry ever attempted to discover if the introduction of prophylactic measures would be useful is very doubtful, as indicated by a Colonial Office memo late in August, 1943 to the effect that the Ministry was *"not doing enough to combat disease... written propaganda is useless as many cannot read English."* (Some could not even speak English.) The Colonial Office advocated the use of films. But this suggestion came too late, as did the suggestion for improving the medical service, for the men's health, and especially the incidence of VD (there were no allegations that VD incapacitated the men), was one of the excuses used by the Ministry for sending the men home before the expiration of their contracts.

Welfare

During 1942 the Colonial Office's Welfare Officers continued their visits to the camps and their pressure on the Ministry of Supply to improve conditions. They interested the British Council and the Colonial Comforts Fund in the plight of the Hondurans, so that recreational material, some sports equipment and musical instruments began to arrive at the camps; by the end of the year the YMCA[3] had established canteens in the southern camps.

Also as a result of Colonial Office pressure, the Ministry in July, 1942 appointed a welfare officer to the British Honduran Forestry Unit. Major Steuart, the new Officer, described by Mr Keith as *"elderly, deaf, but shrewd and honest"*, resigned within five months of his appointment because *"he has no support from Headquarters and is unable to get things done"*. Two new Welfare Officers were appointed, Captain W. Cheyne-Macpherson for the southern camps and a Barbadian, Mr Vivian Harris for the northern camps.

With the help of the Welfare Officers and continuing pressure from the Colonial Office, life in the camps improved. Mr Harris's untiring efforts provided the men, within a couple of months of his appointment, with recreation huts equipped with libraries, pianos and some other musical instruments. He set up camp shops, arranged for film screenings and initiated classes in literacy, maths and English.

Administration

In both the southern and northern camps conditions fluctuated according to the qualities of the camp managers appointed by the Ministry of Supply. The Ministry's official Report on the British Honduras Forestry Unit, dated May 1st 1944, admitted that *"it was impossible to obtain the right stamp of men at the salary offered (£335p.a.)... none of the various Camp Managers appointed can be said to have been fully satisfactory... at four of the camps there were ten changes in management"*. Besides being inadequate managers, the attitude of at least one of these men towards the workers was clearly racialist: *"these men, who have much of the child in their composition, often found it genuinely impossible, when charged with avoidable absenteeism after a lapse of weeks to say whether they had in fact been absent on the day in question"*, the unnamed manager of the Duns camp wrote in December, 1942.

The Ministry's 1944 Report attempts to lay the blame for the maladministration of the Unit on the shoulders of the Officer-in-Charge. Mr Robertson is described in the Report as *"inefficient ... a timber contractor in a comparatively small way of business in the Colony... his main failings were a complete lack of drive and absolute ignorance of the elements of organisation... His only value to the Department was... his advice... when up against the various idiosyncracies of the different races of which the contingents were composed"*. These allegations against Mr Robertson was refuted by his nephew! *"My uncle went to British Honduras after World War I"*, Mr Robertson's nephew wrote to me in April, 1981, *"and established a well-organised and viable buiness in the mahogany trade. He mapped large areas of the hinterland himself and discovered several Maya sites... Timber was felled and removed by caterpillar tractors to the railhead of* a small railway which he and his men had build through the bush...I believe that the bulk of the workforce (for the southern camps) was made up from my uncle's personnel in British Honduras ... I know that my uncle had a lot of trouble with the Ministry of Supply in trying to get warm clothing for his men and enabling them to settle down in other ways in a strange country... My uncle was Justice of the Peace for the Stann Creek and Toledo Districts (in Belize)..." This description of Mr Robertson is at considerable variance with the Ministry's; given the Newfoundlanders' and the Colonial Office's complaints regarding the Ministry's inefficiency, it is, I think, more likely that the Ministry was attempting to protect itself by impugning Mr Robertson. (Mr Robertson died in Belize after the war.)

The southern camps were administered from Edinburgh; for the northern camps a District Office was set up in Dingwall, but *"this office was never satisfactory mainly due to personnel difficulties"*, the Ministry admitted in its official report.

Conditions in the Camps

The League of Coloured Peoples visited the British Honduran Forestry Unit in October/November 1941. They found that in a camp for 180 men, there was only one wash-house with four showers. The nearest bus-stop two miles distant and the only other mode of transport was two bicycles! A protest about conditions in the southern camps was sent to the Colonial Office during 1942.

In December 1942, Mr Keith found the Duns camp to be *"dirty and sordid... a sea of mud"*; the men were having to use packing-cases for furniture in their sleeping huts; the recreation hut annexe at Kirkpatrick Fleming was still unfinished in February 1943, and ENSA had announced that visits would be discontinued because the *"rough conditions will injure the delicate mechanism of their machines"* (film projectors). Mr Keith thought conditions in both camps to be a *"public scandal"*. Despite these conditions and the frequent changes in camp management, Captain Cheyne-Macpherson, the Welfare Officer, has some success: he started literary and debating societies, arranged for local teachers to hold English and maths classes and managed to acquire enough instruments for the men at Duns to form a jazz band. As no instructors were available, some of the men took correspondence classes in motor engineering and various other subjects with a number of institutes.

A more personal glimpse of the camps and the men they housed is given by Dr S.K. Drainer, Deputy Medical Officer of Health in Dumfries (the town nearest to Kirkpatrick Fleming camp) during the war: *"In my opinion, the conditions of the camp were not satisfactory. The huts were of wood and without insulation... The men complained always of the cold — even in what passes for summer in these climes! At the same time, these were war-time conditions, and were no worse than members of the armed forces had to endure by way of dormitary accommodation, ablutions, dining and recreational facilities ... I have the impression that no matter how well-housed or well-clothed they were, they would still be less able to withstand the climatic conditions of war-time Britain than would the indigenous population".* (correspondence, October, 1980)

Work

The Hondurans were employed at a weekly wage of £3, from which 25/- (£1.25) was deducted for board and lodging. This was the wage agreed by the Forestry Commission for unskilled labour, i.e., it was the minimum wage for the timber industry, and was at the bottom end of the wage-scale for unskilled labour, which varied from 52/- to 76/- (£2.60 to £3.80). It is very difficult to understand, unless one presumes that the Ministry of Supply thought of all *"coloured"* men as unskilled, why men in various categories of skill (axemen, sawyers, millwrights, cooks, medical orderlies, etc.) were paid the minimum wage for unskilled labour. (Despite such low wages, by March, 1942, £6,000 per month was being remitted by the men to their families in British Honduras.) There is very little evidence as to what kind of work the men actually did. A report for July, 1942 states that the men were engaged in pitwood felling and sawing, in the manufacture of pit-props and in *"assisting the operations of No's One and Three Australian Forestry Companies"* In December 1942, the men at Kirkpatrick Fleming were *"being employed to do much rougher work for the more high-skilled Australians... this worked alright with No. One Company, but with No. Three relations were much less happy".* Mr McCune, the Duke of Buccleuch's Chief Forester at the time, remembers the Hondurans working on the Duke's property as being *"amenable, quiet-spoken... wanted to get on with the job... they may have had a certain skill, but were classed as labourers... they didn't get along with the Australians at all well... the Australians seemed to look down on them... the Duchess thought the Australians were rather harsh with them".*

In 1943, the League of Coloured Peoples reported that the men in the northern camps were working up to ten miles from the station, *"often on precarious hillsides"*, while the Canadians there had *"jobs within easy reach of the railway station".* Whatever the problems were, they resulted in a go-slow policy which developed into a strike by thirty men on September 18th 1942. The Conciliation Officer was called in and persuaded the men to accept the UK grievance procedures and return to work. He reported on September 22nd that the Hondurans were *"principally employed indirectly as labourers to craftsmen who are members of the Australian Expeditionary Force".* I have not been able to discover what the outcome of the *"grievance procedure"* was; nowhere, however, is there a mention of any of the Hondurans ever receiving craftsmen's wages.

The Ministry of Supply's 1944 Report states that besides working for the Australians, the Hondurans were also engaged in completing and building of their camps and on *"clearing up and finishing certain operations started by the Newfoundland Forestry Unit."* The production during the winter months of 1941/1942 was on a very low level... in April 1942 the men were gradually put on to piece-work. Production started to increase and continued to do so until disciplinary powers (fines for bad work) were taken away... These powers were considered by legal authority to be *"ultra vires".* An undated Ministry report for 1943 calls the *"men of colour fundamentally lazy"* and found the men *"need the influence of discipline to get them to produce their maximum".*

The Ministry produced endless volumes of figures demonstrating that the production of the British Honduran Forestry Unit was below that of other Forestry Units — a result they attributed to laziness and lack of disciplinary powers, but which might well be thought to result from bad management, bad living conditions, low and inappropriate pay, few recreational opportunities, unaccustomed working conditions, unfamiliar work and the racialist attitude of Ministry officials. It should also be noted that the military companies had vastly superior equipment and were allocated to areas where timber was more easy to cut.

It must be mentioned in this context that by June 1943, twenty men had *"absconded"* from their camps and sought alternative work in Cardiff, Manchester, Liverpool and Tyneside. The Ministry was all for having these men arrested and repatriated for breaking their contracts (at a time of immense labour shortage in Britain!); the Colonial Office advised that the *"deserters"* should either be sent to the Government Training Centres (a war-time emergency measure for training in basic engineering skills) or given temporary employment. What actually happened to these *"deserters"* is unrecorded.

vi. RELATIONS WITH THE LOCAL COMMUNITY

The Ministry's recruitment demand that Honduran *"officers"* should be *"white men... This is most important as we must respect, not only the feelings of the proprietors of the estates on which these men are camped, but we must also consider the feelings of people living in surrounding villages"* presupposed that there would be hostility expressed towards black workers by the local communities.

South-West Scotland

The Ministry's hypothesis was not altogether incorrect and some Ministry officials and certain public figures might well be seen as actually fostering animosity towards the Hondurans.

The Duke of Buccleuch in August 1942, wrote directly to Harold Macmillan, then Under-Secretary of State for the

Colonies, about the Hondurans in his fiefdom: *"Does the Colonial Office have any policy about their association with white women?"* he asked. *"There have been a number of marriages and births and much intercourse is allowed even in the camp itself. Personally, I dislike this mixture of colour... there are already sufficient births of foreign extraction without the added complication of colour."* The Colonial Office felt obliged to investigate a Duke's allegations, and found one marriage, no births, no intercourse in the camp (Kirkpatrick Fleming) and no complaints from local residents. But the Duke was not to be pacified so easily: *"I think it can be admitted that loose relations between black men of totally different standards, both moral and material, and our simple country girls has unpleasant features and that improper intercourse with decent young women should be strongly discouraged".* Mr Macmillan's reply was equally racialist in tone: *"it is, of course, obvious that if you bring coloured men to this country for war purposes, there will naturally be the risk of some undesirable results... All we can do is mitigate the evil '.*

Though the local people might well have regarded the *"undesirable results"* of the men's presence as *"evil",* only one complaint about the men's presence in the area is recorded by the Colonial Office. On September 18th, 1941 the files note that *"at Kirkpatrick the local publicans are not too keen on the British Hondurans because the public houses are too small".*

The Duchess appears to be less prejudiced than her husband. In the true style of manorial patronage, visited the men and arranged for regular visits from the factor. Mr McCune, the Chief Forester remembers that *"several of the local girls tried to make the men feel at home... took them honey and home-baked bread and scones... their mothers went along too... it was all on the level... The men amused themselves by playing musical instruments and singing."*

Sir Harold Carrington, the Deputy Director of the Home-Grown Timber Department in Scotland, held similar attitudes to the Duke. He busied himself with *"endeavouring to notify the parents and Ministers and pointing out the undesirability of such marriages"* and reported in July, 1943 that Dumfriesshire County Council had complained about *"discipline in the camps and VD ... one specific complaint put forward was that attendance of these coloured men at the VD clinic was acting as a deterrent on other patients attending"* The Minutes of the Dumfriesshire

Council do indicate that they had held a lengthy correspondence with the Scottish Home, Education and Health Departments on *"certain matters arising out of the residence of coloured workmen in the County"*, but as the correspondence itself has not been retained either in Edinburgh or Dumfries, it has not been possible to ascertain the nature of the complaints (or suggestions: the Departments of Health and Education could in no way be in a position to entertain complaints about the Hondurans). Dr Drainer, the Deputy Medical Officer of Health, was in charge of the VD clinic and categorically refutes the allegation that the Hondurans prevented other patients attending: *"this small Centre, which was quite adequate to serve the needs of the civilian population locally in peacetime was, by 1941, in process of being swamped by civilian cases, members of the armed forces and men from the camp and Kirkpatrick Fleming. To begin with the Hondurans attended along with all the others but, when their numbers increased, it seemed only reasonable that a day should be set aside for them. . . As they were brought to Dumfries, attendances were regular. . . I think they looked upon their weekly trip to Dumfries as a sort of outing — a pleasure not shared by the County Clerk, who objected strenuously to their sunning themselves on fine days in front of the County Buildings."* Dr Drainer remembers *"three children born to women in the vicinity of the camp whose putative fathers were from the camp"*. This number — and we don't know if the mothers married the *"putative fathers"* — does not seem very high in a country where illegitimacy and according to the special judicial Report for 1939-1945 *"has always been unduly high, sometimes approximating to double the rate for Scotland"*. This report also deals with VD: the numbers of new cases had risen from 50 in 1939 to 236 in 1943, and 231 in 1945; the reasons given for this increase are: the presence of troops, female camp-followers and *"the establishment of a camp of negro foresters, so many of whom were found to be infected that a special day had to be arranged for dealing with them"*. (It should be noted that Dr Drainer's clinic was not given extra staff to deal with this increase in the numbers of its patients. The acute shortage of medical and laboratory staff for the civilian population during the war was exacerbated by certain civilian clinics having also to cater for military personnel.)

One is left wondering as to how the Hondurans were to conduct themselves: *"decent"* girls were warned to stay away from them, while if they consorted with prostitutes and contracted VD they met with opprobrium. Mr Keith of the Colonial Office understood the situation well: the Hondurans: *"immoralities get more publicity"*, he wrote early in 1943, *"and are more shocking to the susceptibilities of persons like the Duke of Buccleuch and his friends than would be the goings-on of non-coloured persons"*. Mr Whitehorn, also of the Colonial Office, concurred with Mr Keith that *"Carrington is the villain of the piece... Not only has he shown the most regrettable lethargy in regard to the administration of the camps, but he has been guilty of petty chicanery in regard to one of the foresters"*. (Unfortunately the file dealing with this *"petty chicanery"* has not been preserved at the Public Records Office.)

South East Camps

The Hondurans and at least some sections of the local population seem to have started off *"on the wrong foot"* in this part of Scotland. Mr I. Cummings of the Colonial Office's welfare team noted on October 30th, 1941 that *"following some unpleasantness in East Linton, sexual and alcoholic, a deputation of local Ministers of the Kirk suggested that the villages of East Linton and Duns should be put out of bounds."* Mr Keith, however, minuted that *"putting the villages out-of-bounds is quite unnecessary . . . the men have established happy relations with the local people and are popular with them. There have been one or two unpleasant incidents, but nothing that need cause us concern."*

By the end of November the panic in the Church had subsided: the Presbytery of Duns Minutes record that *"Mr Douglas reported on the presence in the district of lumbermen from British Honduras and the work the Church should do for them"*. The Stenton Kirk Sessions for January 14th, 1942 noted that *"the moderator intimated that with the co-operation of the Minister of Whittinghame a weekly service was being held at the British Honduras camp which is in this parish"*. The present Minister in Stenton, who has very kindly made enquiries among his congregation, discovered that Dr Mackenzie, one of his predecessors at Stenton, *"came to the camp every Sunday night and took a service for the men . . . He and his wife were thought to have exercised some kind of pastoral concern for them . . . Obviously, there was *some initial reserve amongst the folk of East Lothian when the Hondurans came. But there were not so very many of them, and my older parishioners who remember them speak well of them. They were friendly and in some cases talented. One, Jimmy Christie, was invited by the Minister of Spott to play his trumpet at local kirk and village soirees. My impression is that they were respected locally, and that some people felt sorry for them since they were so far from home . . . No doubt illegitimacy in a few cases might have caused ill feeling . . . but the overall reaction does not seem to have been hostile."*

Mrs James of Bielgrange remembers that *"some of the men visited in homes on the farm and were welcomed, but other local people prided themselves on keeping apart. Those who remember Hondurans at local dances say that they were well-behaved . . . Involvement of local girls with Hondurans was generally frowned on".* Mrs Trueman, who worked in an approved school in the area, writes that she *"did not come into any contact with them, so what I know is hearsay . . . I used to hear of the fellows having parties, etc . . . there were two black babies — one causing a divorce!! I believe both girls married their Hondurans who have proved kind husbands (so far as I know). The consensus of opinion locally at the time was that it was the 'camp-followers' who got most of the blame . . ."*

It appears that while some local girls had ambivalent attitudes towards the men, other women[4] were quite happy to associate with them. The Ministry strongly disapproved, saying the men's sleeping quarters were Crown property from which trespassers could be removed; the men at Duns maintained that they had the right to have overnight guests. This contretemps became one of the main topics of discussion at a Ministry of Supply conference on November 17th, 1942, when the Ministry of Supply noted that there had been *"two cases of immoral relations with women outside the camps in circumstances giving rise to local scandal . . . it was considered that while the Department* (i.e., the Home Grown Timber Department) *could regard itself as free from any responsibility in such cases where Europeans were concerned, it could not do so where coloured persons were involved."* This racialist *"concern"* resulted in two police raids on the Duns camp when: *"a number of women were found and apprehended"*; eighteen *"troublemakers were also found in the camp loafing"*. It was recommended that these eighteen should be immediately repatriated; the women were imprisoned for trespassing on government property. The Colonial Office's welfare officers investigated these events and found that before the raids *"undesirable women had defied the efforts of the police and the manager to remove them . . . women are alleged to come up from South Shields to 'visit' Duns"*. The Ministry's 1944 Report allegation that while on leave, *"the men tended to lodge in most undesirable quarters"* was most likely and unavoidably true as the men were not admitted into the Services' leave hostels, could not afford hotels, and the Ministry had done nothing to provide leave facilities. The Colonial Office stepped into this breach: a leave hostel run by the YMCA for Hondurans was opened in Edinburgh in May, 1943, and another in Inverness in August of the same year.

The Reverend Kenneth Hughes of Linton, a local historian for whose invaluable help I am most grateful, sums up local people's attitudes as: *"it is quite difficult to construct any accurate and factual picture of the true situation, disentangled from the myths that exist after forty years. On balance I would say that the local community did quite well in respect of the men. There was hostility and suspicion but it was not, I think, just as a result of rampant unthinking colour-bar. Had the Black Watch of the Argyle and Sutherland Highlanders been situated locally the same kind of feelings would have arisen . . . Some of the men were thought to be very talented in several directions and they made specific contacts with the local community, either through the medium of entertainment* (the Colonial Office reports show that the jazz band from the Duns camp played at local dances) *or at athletics . . . More personal contacts did take place on a quite friendly and innocent level. These tended to be frowned upon, and to be open to misconstruction, and were the exception rather than the rule . . . The local community were scandalised by the 'camp-followers'. This unsettled the local populace and their womenfolk, although after forty years, condemnation of the 'camp-followers' far exceeds condemnation of the men . . . The racial, colour element and related myths obviously played a part in determining local reactions: suspicion, fear, conflict of natural kindliness being confused with 'camp-followers', the unfamiliarity of the 'darkies' (as they were referred to, not uncharitably, and certainly not with the contempt of the epithet 'niggers'*[5] *. . . one has to remember an East Lothian of forty years ago with many of the men at war, the rest workers on the land for generations, not given much to travel outside their own area, and innately conservative in attitude."*

The Northern Camps

No government documents pertaining to these camps are in existence and only one reader has responded to my plea for information in the local papers. Mrs Harrison of Kildonan in Sutherland has written saying that she was *"sitting my sixth-year examinations. I used to serve in my father's sweet shop and I remember studying Omar Khayyam and being most surprised when this black man spoke and quoted lines from this poem. He was Bill Lightburn and was to become one of our many friends... The men came to the village of Golspie in 1943. Very soon these lads were accepted by us ... They lived some distance out of Golspie. They had their own football team and played against the Golspie boys. They regularly attended Church services ... I can recall vividly the Sunday morning when they left Golspie by special train — I could say the whole village was at the station to bid them farewell and sorry to see them go."*

vii. REPATRIATION

Though Dr Patterson and sixteen men described as *"bad hats"* were suggested for repatriation as early as May, 1942, only Dr Patterson and nine men, of whom four were ill, were returned home when shipping was finally found in September, 1942. Whether the eighteen men *"found loafing"* in camp during the December, 1942 police raids were repatriated then, or if they were included in the 130 or so *"undesirable characters"* the Ministry wanted *"to get rid of"* in April, 1943 is unclear. Besides its major concern over the Hondurans' association with white women, the Ministry's other reasons for advocating repatriation only some five months after the second contingent's arrival (and only nineteen months after the arrival of the first) were twofold: the Hondurans were held to be very uneconomic producers and the Ministry felt that it had lost all *"possibility of exercising any real control over the men"* since the Lord Advocate's ruling that to fine them was illegal.

    Mr Keith's riposte of a memorandum in response to the

Ministry's note advocating repatriation read: "... *the real issue is that the Unit never had firm and sympathetic leadership. Supply has been pressed to re-organise leadership to no avail*". He disagreed with the Ministry's notion that discipline was dependent on penalties, suggesting that it depended on leadership. *"There is no real evidence"*, his memo to the Under-Secretary continues, *"that the Unit behaves in a worse way than the Newfoundlanders and other foreigners in Scotland, but they are coloured men and their immoralities get more publicity."*

By June, 1943 the Duke of Devonshire, Under-Secretary of State for the Colonies since January, 1943, found the Ministry's request to repatriate 130 men quite *"unacceptable"*. Nevertheless, bowing to pressure from the Ministry, the Duke two months later consented to repatriating 97 men who, according to the Ministry, had agreed to return. The 93 men who were reported to have sailed by the beginning of August included *"28 medical cases, 24 whose physique could not stand the climate"*, 20 axemen for whom there was no suitable employment, 12 who had been in trouble with the police and others described variously as *"bad worker"*, *"lazy and an agitator"* and *"persistent absentee"*:[6]

Not satisfied with this, or perhaps because they scented victory, the Ministry returned to the hunt a few days after the men had sailed: *"if they can be spared, they should be returned home"*, the Ministry wrote to the Duke on August 10th, citing the men's health as the main reason for wanting to repatriate. The Ministry asked the Duke to discuss the issue. Mr Keith tried to arm his Under-Secretary for the forthcoming meeting: *"the immediate pretext for the proposal is the stated large number of VD cases"*, he wrote, *"but VD is preventable and curable"*. He advocated that *"a special officer who has knowledge of this disease in its incidence upon non-Europeans should if possible be appointed to make an examination of the whole question in all the camps"*; and that propaganda to combat the disease should be increased. Mr Keith went on to warn the Duke that repatriation *"would be deplorable and could only be justified if the Unit were worthless from the production point of view ... if General Carrington feels unable to cope with the administration, let us propose replacing him ... Apart from the fact that a great deal of money has been spent putting up camps and in bringing the men over here, their return home would, I imagine, have a very discouraging effect in the West Indies and would expose the Colonial Office, as well as the Ministry, to a good deal of criticism . . . The principal reason against repatriating these men is the most unfortunate politica consequences which would result . . . The problem of absorbing some 850 men into employment in British Honduras is bound to present difficulties."*

Another Colonial Office official presented additional arguments: *". . . if the British Honduran men are sent back and the New Zealand men are kept we shall have cries of colour discrimination which would perhaps not be easy to answer.*[7] *It seems to me that the Ministry of Supply really want to send the men back because they have mismanaged the whole show and want to cover up before it's too late. The Dominions Office has had to make constant efforts to prod the Ministry of Supply into making proper arrangements for the Newfoundlanders."* He and numerous other officials thought that the Ministry's proposal to repatriate should be *"fought vigorously"*.

Mr Cummings, who had spoken with General Carrington in Edinburgh on September 2nd, prophesied that *"the higher authority at Shell Mex House (the Ministry's headquarters) are determined to make us accept the repatriation position and I think we shall find that they are going to use the argument that the need for production no longer justifies the employment of British Hondurans"*. His prediction came true at the meeting on September 8th, when the Duke accepted the Ministry's contention that reserves of standing timber were being depleted and that the supply of imported timber was increasing.[8] *"It was common ground that there were problems with the Hondurans"*, the Ministry claimed, and *"people of the neighbourhood (of the three southern camps) would be relieved by the return of the men."* The Duke capitulated: repatriation was agreed, with only two small provisos: The Governor's views should be solicited and the Ministry of Labour consulted over the *"absorption of men who might wish to stay"*.

It is not clear from the records how many men were eventually repatriated. What is clear is that there were problems over how to return the men to British Honduras. The United States, which had previously been used as a staging post, at first refused to comply with a repeat request because of the debacle over the August, 1943 repatriations. The 93 men then being returned home had arrived in New York on the **SS Queen Elizabeth** without passports or visas, with numerous cases of VD and TB (people with infectious diseases are not allowed into the US) and with no arrangements for their onward travel to Belize. Thus being illegal immigrants, the men were imprisoned on Ellis Island until the British Consul arranged for them to travel to British Honduras overland. The irate Consul had to provide the men with warm clothing and pocket-money as they had arrived only with clothing suitable for the tropics and their month-long imprisonment had exhausted their funds. However, on receiving assurances that this time all the necessary paperwork had been done, that all the men had warm clothing and medical certificates and that onward travel had been arranged, the US agreed for the men to sail to New York, travel by train to New Orleans and from there by ship to Belize.

viii. THE MEN WHO REMAINED

At the end of December, 1943, 268 men were still in the UK, though I believe many of them later returned to British Honduras. Some of those who remained found jobs for themselves with small local firms; others, who turned to the Ministry of Labour experienced considerable delays in being found employment, despite the war-time labour shortage. Rolls-Royce, a large employer in the area, told the Ministry of Labour that they expected that *"home labour"* would shortly become available; despite the Ministry of Labour refuting this, Rolls used to employ Hondurans. ICI, another large local employer, refused the men on the basis that their head office had vetoed them. Men were eventually found jobs with British Aluminium, the railways, the Scottish Motor Transport Company and in the merchant marine.

The armed services were no more enthusiastic about taking the Hondurans. Some men were apparently accepted by the Royal Navy, sworn in, only to be told at the last minute that they could not be taken. Mr Cummings, investigating this, spoke with Mr Ryder in the Admiralty and reported that *"the Admiralty felt that colonial coloured volunteers were rather an embarrassment and difficult to place in this country"*. Regretfully, after further discussions, at the end of December, Messrs Keith and Cummings decided that they had to *"accept the position . . . it was the same story with the RAF"*.[9]

ix. THE MEN WHO RETURNED

Other than in a note in the League of Coloured People's **Newsletter** for September, 1944 that members of the British Honduran Forestry Unit had written to the Secretary of State for the Colonies protesting about lack of employment in British Honduras and the Secretary's reply that arrangements were being made for employment in the US (1,241 were working there by December), the only information I have about the men who returned to Belize comes from the Scottish wife of one of the men, who has recently returned to Scotland after 32 years residence in Belize.

Mrs Pearl Waters[10] was one of the fourteen Scottish wives who accompanied their husbands to British Honduras. Mrs Waters describes herself as having been very young and innocent when she met her husband: *"I never used to go round with boys . . . I was 17 . . . They had dances up there* (the British Honduras Forestry Unit camp), *they had their own band, but I never used to go . . . Then they see me go with him and then I'm going to be married to him. I was the talk of the village: there's only one reason I'm marrying him — because there's something wrong with me — foolishness — but that's expected . . . I used to go courting with him openly, I never hide it. I know the villagers never liked it because to them I was a nice little girl . . . a nice little girl in the village and I never go nowhere and they never hear nothing about me and it came as a shock . . . You're supposed to be a disgrace when you married a coloured person . . . People looked down on him because of his colour."*

Despite her family's disapproval, the couple married; young Pearl was told that "(she'd) made (her) bed, (she'd) have to lie in it". Looking back, Mrs Water doesn't *"know how I got involved — but I get in — you're romantic and you get foolish ideas . . . you're young and you don't realise the realities of life"*.

The young couple stayed in the family home and husband Ernest found work with local firms until 1947 when they left for British Honduras. *"He never wanted to go back, you know, back to his home. I encouraged him to go back because I felt he'd have a better chance working over there than here, though he had a good job with Laing's, the contractors. They never wanted him to go . . . In those days, you know, they had this prejudice — you* know, this coloured and coloured and coloured . . . More prejudiced against the coloured men than against the Poles or the Italians. It was the colour more than anything else . . . the men were aware of that. I thought . . . you know, there's jobs over there in his country, that's coloured — the majority is coloured . . ."*

But Mrs Waters' dreams were not realised: her husband was unable to obtain work in Belize; they went to his native village where at least they could grow their own food and where the Waters family welcomed the young Scottish girl and helped her settle down. Mr Waters sought work all over British Honduras — *"we went up the river by canoe . . . then to St. George's Cay — the hurricane caught us there. That he had work experience in Britain made no difference. He was disappointed and he wanted to come back 'home' but we couldn't make it back. I think all that made him despondent . . . he was despondent and he started to drink and then he got sick and he wouldn't listen to the doctor and carried on drinking and that . . . and then he got crippled and couldn't work."*

"I never worked until he started to take sick . . . I heard of a vacancy and I went straightaway and the (British) Army asked why I wanted the job because it's not such a nice job (cleaning) — I said I know." The Army doctors helped Mrs Waters nurse her husband, who nevertheless soon died of bronchial pneumonia. The Army then helped Mrs Waters to return to her native village of Kretna. As the Waters had had no children, Mrs Waters left only her husband's relatives in Belize, who were *"old you know . . . they said to me they were glad I was going home, back to my own people . . . My mother-in-law was living with me before I came and I never wanted to leave her — but I couldn't bring her. Where would I put her? My husband's family really cared for me. I like it over there, but his family said 'here if we die we don't know what would happen to you'."* So Mrs Waters is back in Kretna, where most of her family are dead and few friends remain. *"That's a thing of the past",* her patronising old friends say to her, *"forget it, that's something that's past now and you can't do anything about it. Don't let it spoil your future . . . They talk to me and that . . . But I keep more to myself. I sort of afraid to make friends with people. I think I'm lonely."*

Of the fourteen wives who went to British Honduras, *"most came back . . . The novelty wore off, the novelty of going over there ... They didn't like the life there ... The government sent them back home ... One of the girls had servants and all, her husband get her a girl to help her ... There's another girl — she married just before we — she come over with the girls and her husband come over with her. And then about three years ago she went back over to Belize with her husband, and she's over there now. They have a shop and everything there. She doesn't want to come back."*

x. CONCLUSIONS

That racism and racialism are not related to the numbers of Black people in the country or to economic recessions is amply demonstrated by the foregoing. At a time of serious labour shortage and great emphasis on the need for solidarity in the struggle against the enemy, the presence of a very small group of Black workers imported from the colonies led to manifestations of institutional racism and personal racialism, especially among officials. Though many villagers, especially in the Highlands, extended hospitality to the strangers in their midst, associations between the Hondurans and the village girls were not accepted. Those women who defied this ban and married Hondurans were usually ostracised by their families.

In the colonies the government prevented Blacks from participating in public life as full citizens and from attaining recognition as skilled or professional workers by the use of the 'colour bar'. In the UK the same tactics could not be employed. While publicly decrying the existence of colour bars, the government used discriminatory wages, employment, living and working conditions, and total non-recognition of skills to achieve the same aims: the black man could be nothing other than a beast of burden.[11] And some, such as General Carrington, attempted to ensure that those who strayed from this view should be returned to the racialist view he advocated.

Thus, despite the need for labour, when the racialist horror of miscegenation (as expressed in the hysteria over marriages and the incidence of VD) was combined with the fear of the 'beast' getting out of control (as expressed in alarm at the loss of disciplinary powers), all the Ministries concerned agreed to a hasty repatriation.

A question remains to be asked:

Given that neither the Forestry Commission nor the Ministry of Supply wanted 'coloured labour' in the country, why were the men brought to Scotland? One can only surmise that there was considerable pressure from the Colonial Office on the Ministry of Supply to use the Hondurans. The Colonial Office might well have seen this as a solution to problems in Belize: by September, 1940, 1,820 Hondurans were 'on relief' and the Governor was asking for 'subsidies from England'. It is also likely that there were political considerations at stake: the Royal Commission investigating conditions throughout the British West Indies had found the people's grievances, which had led to the 1937 wave of 'riots' justified. The Commission's Report was felt to be such an indictment of British neglect of the Caribbean islands that its publication was suppressed by the British government until 1945; the Commission's recommendations were published, but the outbreak of war conveniently prevented much action having to be taken. In fact, conditions worsened to such an extent that starvation was feared by a number of governors. The British Government's investment in heavy pro-'mother-country' propaganda had to be stepped up, especially when German propaganda began to sweep the islands. In these dircumstances, it is arguable that the Colonial Office sought to at least partially solve the problems in Belize by using unemployed Honduran labour in Britain.

The Ministries of Supply and Labour, faced with increasing labour shortages as the war progressed, probably acceded to the Colonial Office's request despite their prejudices towards 'coloured labour' in the hope of alleviating labour supply problems. However, by the stringencies of the employment contracts, the Ministries obviously hoped to contain the men within strict confines. When this didn't work, when the men struck for the pay they were entitled to as skilled workers or refused to work because of bad conditions or lack of equipment, they were labelled 'bad hats; lazy; agitator', and repatriated. (There must naturally have been a few unsuitable men among the 900 brought to Britain: it is not known what selection procedures were used and the Governor might well have seized the opportunity to rid the colony of men he saw as troublemakers.)

The Ministry of Supply, even given war-time shortages, blatantly did the very minimum to provide conditions in which the men could work. Barely furnished, uninsulated and unheated barracks, no hot water, insufficient warm clothing, no recreational or leave facilities, labouring wages, numerous isolated camps, the misuse of their skills and maladministration at all levels were not guarantees for a happy workforce. Once could almost say that what the Ministry set about ensuring was that the Hondurans would be 'bad producers' in order to vindicate its final judgement that 'coloured labour recruited into the UK can only be justified as a dire necessity'.

The Colonial Office's Welfare Department, understaffed and powerless, could do little to improve matters. And what they did do was usually an emergency measure to stem the tide of Supply's complaints. The Duke of Devonshire evidently did not, at the meeting with the Ministry on September 8th, live up to his welfare staff's request to fight repatriation 'vigorously'. The tardiness and inadequacies of the Welfare Department could be interpreted as indicating that their and the Colonial Office's real concern was not the plight of the Hondurans in Britain, but the control of the Empire.

NOTES

1. Unless indicated otherwise, quotations in the text are taken from government files listed in 'References'.

2. Russell Meiggs, who had been Chief Labour Officer with the Home Grown Timber Department, in his book *Home Timber Production* (1949) felt obliged to explain at length why the Australian and New Zealand production output fell below that of the Canadians: the Australians and New Zealanders were used to working at speed without regard to "the strict economy in felling and cutting" necessary during war; "British trees and particularly hardwoods are also of very mixed quality and special selection and treatment is required". Meiggs gives no such explanation when writing of the lower output of the Newfoundland and British Honduran units; neither does he mention the vast difference in techniques required for cutting mahogany and British hardwoods.

3. As the League of Coloured Peoples reported (citing their evidence) on their May, 1941 **News Notes** that the YMCA discriminated against black people, one is left to wonder why the Colonial Office chose the YMCA to run canteens for Afro-Caribbeans.

4. The report, **Behaviour of Girls and Young Women in Wartime** (1942) by the Chief Constable of Glasgow, appears to be an expression of concern at what was obviously seen as a loosening of morals: *'In the early autumn of 1940 this (concentration of troops) became more of a problem and it was apparent that many young women and girls were parading the streets in company with men of the various services including the different nationals...'*

5. This notion, held by so many, that women associating with blacks could only be *'camp-followers'* was not peculiar to the 1940s; in 1930, M.E. Fletcher, investigating the **Colour Problem in Liverpool and other Ports**, wrote: *'90% of the white women in Liverpool who consort with coloured men are said to be prostitutes... the white women in Liverpool who consort with coloured men... are mentally weak, prostit-*

utes (or) younger women who make contacts in a spirit of adventure and find themselves unable to break away'. Miss Fletcher also found that *'these women will say that they married a coloured man because he makes a better husband than a white. Such a statement appears to be merely an excuse . . . they almost invariably regret their alliance . . . the white woman who consorts with coloured men is very conscious of having ostracised herself. . . her parents will have nothing to do with her. . . They cannot be seen about with their husbands. . .'* It seems that the fear or horror of miscegenation was never far beneath the surface of *'natural kindliness'* and that this fear strongly influenced both personal and official attitudes and behaviour.

6. Reasons for absenteeism were apparently never investigated by the Ministry. A brief article in the **Dumfries and Galloway Standard** of 26/12/42 throws some light on this: B.H. Alton Brown is reported as being fined £10 (or 40 days imprisonment) for being absent from work for 46 days). Mr Alton Brown claimed that he had torn his shoes in August despite numerous requests for a new pair he had not been given any until October. The Camp Manager's confirmation that there hadn't been any shoes in the camp store had little influence with the magistrate. It should also be remember that Hondurans were used to working six months of the year. To adjust to working twelve months a year is no easy matter. It is curious to note that except for another court report, I can find no mention of the Hondurans in the Scottish papers, though the Newfoundlanders and the military companies were mentioned on numerous occasions. That writing about the Hondurans was censored is a possibility: there is a note in CO968/38 to the effect that the **Glasgow Herald** and the **Glasgow Bulletin** had interviewed the men on arrival, but that the censor had *'killed'* the story.

7. In fact, the Australian and New Zealand Companies left Scotland at about the same time as the Hondurans, but not to return home: there was an urgent demand for foresters in Algeria, the Mediterranean, Western Europe and New Guinea. Twenty Canadian Companies were still working in Scotland in 1944. There were no public cries of discrimination. Had the censor killed these too?

8. Whether this is strictly true is doubtful: not only were the Canadians retained until 1944, but Italian and German POWs were sent to work in Scotland in 1944 and 1945. Were they cheaper labour than the Hondurans? They were certainly white.

9. Yet the man-power shortage in the armed services was so severe that the Royal Air Force was forced into recruiting five and a half thousand men from the Caribbean in 1944.

10. All my informants' names have been changed to protect their privacy.

11. Just how discriminatory the terms were is high-lighted by the Temporary Workers in Agriculture (Scotland) (Minimum Wages) Order of 1943 (No. 465 S12) which prescribed a wage of 58/- per week for students and other volunteer workers in agriculture and forestry. This was just 2/- per week less than the skilled Hondurans were paid.

REFERENCES

I   **Introduction**
PRO: AVIA 46/486
R. Meiggs: Home Timber Production, 1949.

II.   **British Honduras**
Report of the Committee on Nutrition, Belize Crown Agents, 1937.
Colonial Reports, British Honduras, No. 1894, 1938.
West Indian Royal Commission Report, HMSO, 1945.
British Honduras Blue Book, 1939.

III   **Recruitment**
PRO: CO 123/373   AVIA22/1352
        AVIA46/494   DO35/745
        CO876/41   CO123/378
        CO968/38/2

IV   **Arrival**
        CO968/40   CO876/41
        CO968/38/2   CO876/42

V   **Life in the Camps**
        CO968/38   CO876/43
        CO0876/41   AVIA46/486
League of Coloured Peoples Newsletter, November 1943, p.22.

VI   **Relations with the Local Community**
        CO968/38   CO876/42
        CO876/41   AVIA46/486
Dumfries County Council Special Medical Report, 1939-45.

VII   **Repatriation**
        CO876/42   FO368/2924

4. West Indian Seamen: A Note

WEST INDIAN SEAMEN

Though the Navigation Laws of 1660 prescribed that three-fourths of an English ship's crew must be English, from 1794, because of a shortage of seamen, *"Negroes in the seas of America, belonging to any Person being His Majesty's Subject"* were permitted to crew British ships. Though originally confined to the trade between the West Indies and north America, West Indian seamen made their way to Britain, settling and sailing from Liverpool, Cardiff, Barry, North and South Shields and London. Together with seamen from India, Somalia, Arabia and West Africa, these West Indians formed the nucleus of the Black communities living in Britain's major ports.

The very limited information I have on West Indian seamen during World War II is drawn entirely from the few remaining Colonial Office files, which refer almost exclusively to wartime recruitment in the West Indies. These files do not reveal how many West Indians made their own way to Britain in order to join the merchant marine; nor do they speak of the prejudice encountered by Blacks in the seamen's employment 'pools' where many masters and shipping companies refused to hire them. As my material is so limited, I shall only present a summary of the information.

The files begin November 1939, when the Colonial Office offered the services of West Indian seamen to the Ministry of Shipping. On January 23, 1940 representatives of the Ministry, the Dominions Office, the Colonial Office and the Shipping Federation (the shipowners' cartel) met to discuss the use of West Indian and Newfoundland seamen. The meeting concentrated on Newfoundland as *"Newfoundland men are a much simpler problem because we are not faced with the colour difficulty"*.[1] The Ministry promised the Colonial Office that if West Indians were used, they would be repatriated as soon as possible after the war and that it would *"consider whether the best use of West Indians is a whole crew or as part of a crew on ships sailing between Britain and the West Indies"*.[2]

As a month later the Colonial Office had not heard further from the Ministry, they wrote pressing the case for West Indian employment: *"I need hardly point out to you that the recruit-*

ment of seamen for the Merchant Navy in the West Indies would undoubtedly have an excellent political effect and it would meet to some extent the desire of the people for more active participation in the war, a desire which now appears to be unlikely to be met in any other way. . . . We should take strong exception to anything which looked like an extension of the colour bar. . . ."[3]

Colonial Office internal memoranda show that at least Messrs Mayle and Norris were convinced that "*the colour bar question has a lot to do with their* (the Ministry of Shipping) *attitude*" and that the case should be urged both with the Ministry and the National Union of Seamen, who "*should be pressed to withdraw their objection*" if it was based on colour. However, Colonial Office staff were divided on racial questions, as shown in Mr Williams' memorandum of 21/2/40: "*. . . the plain fact is that the black man smells differently from the white and it is therefore unpleasant for them both to be herded together in close proximity . . . nasty incidents will arise if the matter is pressed . . .*"[4]. The Colonial Office acquiesced, as it did over the munitions workers and the recruitment of West Indians for the armed forces: on May 21st, 1940, telegrams ordered the West Indian governors not to send any West Indian seamen to Britain.

As the next file has been destroyed, we can only surmise that it was high shipping losses which brought about the rescission of the May 1940 decision. On 4/3/41 it was decided to recruit West Indian seamen provided they were repatriated at the end of 12 months' service. However, as repatriation could not be made compulsory, Mr Calder of the Colonial Office, fearing an increase in the Black population in Britain, advised that the Home Office should be warned of the proposal. It was also emphasised that the NUS had only agreed to co-operate if the West Indians were repatriated and if they were not to share quarters with white crew.

In July 1941 the Colonial Office felt obliged to apologise to the West Indian governors for the delay in recruiting seamen. Two months later, that is, six months after the decision to recruit, the Ministry of War Transport (which now included the old Ministry of Shipping) authorised Sir Ashley Sparks, its US representative, to recruit West Indian crews for ships being built by the US for Britain. Recruitment was, however, only to take place if the "*master does not absolutely object*".[5]

It seems the masters did not object, as West Indian crews were recruited for seven American-built ships: the *Oceans Vigil*,

Viking, *Vestal*, *Vesper*, *Valley*, *Vision* and *Liberty*. Complaints were immediately voiced about the men: *"West Indian crews so far obtained from Trinidad have not proved satisfactory"*; *"this crew ... have been most unsatisfactory ... as soon as the officers were out of sight, they stopped working"*; the Ocean *Vestal*'s crew were *"inexperienced, ignorant and insolent"*; the Ocean *Viking* crew were all discharged in Montreal because of *"inefficiency"*.[6] A total of 32 men were immediately repatriated to Trinidad and 13 to Jamaica. Though Sparks reported fewer complaints about crews from Jamaica, he decided on 15/2/42 not to accept any more seamen from the West Indies.

While we do not know whether pressure had to be exerted on the masters and officers of these vessels to accept West Indian seamen, it is clear from the file that certain factors have to be taken into account before we accept the charges against the seamen:

(1) the men had had a long, unpaid wait between being recruited and shipping out
(2) at least the crew of the *Ocean Vigil* had been recruited for an oil-burning ship but found themselves working on a coal-burner
(3) US immigration had interned the *Ocean Vigil*'s crew
(4) there were problems and delays over the payment of allotments to families
(5) there were *"problems over accommodation"* on the *Ocean Vigil*
(6) their terms of employment indicated that the men would not be paid while awaiting repatriation at the end of 12 months' service
(7) some masters, for example for the Moore McCormack line, refused to accept men recruited by their own agents in the West Indies (how widespread this practice was the file does not indicate).

The men might well have had good cause for displaying a certain amount of recalcitrance. It should also be borne in mind that it is quite possible that the masters and officers themselves were inexperienced, given the wartime shortage of experienced sailors and that the West Indians might well not have been experienced in sailing the type of vessel for which they were recruited. Nevertheless, obviously both the Ministry and the Colonial Office accepted the charges against the West Indian seamen as they condoned Sparks' decision to stop recruiting there for the US-built ships.

The Colonial Office files also reveal that:
(1) the men from the *Ocean Vigil* and the *Ocean Liberty* spent at least 10 weeks in the segregated hostel in Newcastle awaiting employment as *"white crews are strongly prejudiced against mixed travelling"*[7]
(2) the British police had not ceased the practice developed in the 1920s of registering West Indian seamen as *"aliens"*, thereby prohibiting them from going ashore on leave[8]
(3) there were reports of the wages of West Indian crews being withheld by masters
(4) despite the National Maritime Board having *"established"* equal wages for white and Black crews shipped from Britain, there were complaints about differential wage rates in certain 'pools'.

It is not surprising therefore that in July 1942 the Colonial Office decided to cease recruiting seamen in Trinidad. That recruitment was also curtailed in the other islands is revealed by the Ministry's reply to a Colonial Office request in June 1944 for help with easing the *"serious unemployment among West Indian seamen"* in both Britain and the Caribbean. They would not again recruit in the Caribbean, the Ministry replied, as *"earlier attempts had not been very successful"*. At a meeting on July 20, 1944, the Colonial Office tried to press the issue by pointing out that 15% of Colonial seamen had lost their lives in enemy action and that UK shipowners recruited from the pools *"to the exclusion of coloured seamen"*, leading to 350 West Indian seamen being unemployed in Liverpool and Cardiff alone.[9] The Ministry promised the *"possibility of employing these men at the rate of 50 per month"*, provided that the Colonial Office arranged their ultimate repatriation. As the Pool Registrars seemingly refused to co-operate in increasing the employment of West Indians, they were offered to the Canadian National Steamship Co. and the US War Shipping Administration.[10] The US refused them on the basis that they had used a few West Indian seamen in 1943 and had found them unsatisfactory.[11] The Canadians not only would not employ more West Indians but even discharged the British Guianese in their employ early in 1945. The Harrison Line however, which already had West Indian crews on four of their ships, agreed to also employ them for the *Empire Chivalry*. As this did not make much of a dent in unemployment among seamen in the Caribbean, their unions continued to ask the Colonial Office to put pressure on the Ministry of War Transport, but to no avail. Until its dissolution, the Ministry adamantly refused to aid the employment of West Indians either in Britain or the Caribbean.

FOOTNOTES AND REFERENCES

1. Ministry of Shipping to the Colonial Office, 30/1/40, in CO318/441/71215.
2. Minutes of meeting held 23/1/40, ibid.
3. Colonial Office to the Ministry of Shipping, 23/2/40, ibid. It should be noted that this letter admits the existence of a colour bar and acknowledges that government policy is not to employ West Indians in the war effort. The Colonial Office was, as always, walking in the narrow path between having to prevent ferment in the colonies and appeasing their anti-Black Cabinet colleagues. That the Colonial Office and its Secretaries of State were not free of racist bias has been amply demonstrated in these essays.
4. Minutes by NL Mayle 7/2/40, 14/2/40 and 1/3/40; by R Norris, 13/2/40; by ? Williams, 21/2/40, ibid.
5. Ministry of War Transport to Sparks, 23/9/41, in CO318/449/71215.
6. Sparks to MWT, 31/1/42; Master C. Bailey of the *Ocean Vigil* to Sparks, 7/2/42; Sparks to MWT, 15/2/42, ibid.
7. The Colonial Office was well aware of segregation in the shipping industry. For instance, Mr CV Minto, the President of the International Coloured Mutual Aid Association of North Shields, in correspondence with the Colonial Office regarding the plight of Black children and the necessity for setting up a social centre and a hostel for Black seamen, noted that North Shields' 200 West Indian seamen were all members of the NUS and while not facing *"a colour bar, faced segregation, which is worse"*. (See CO859/76/12811/6 for the full correspondence between Mr Minto and the Colonial Office. Mr Minto's son Charles was one of a number of British Blacks whom the Royal Navy refused to enlist during the war.)
8. The policy of writing 'coloured' in the space for 'nationality' on seamen's registration papers and thereby issuing British seamen with aliens' papers was developed by the police during the 1920s, in order to prevent their employment. The practice was continued during the '30s. How common it was after the outbreak of war, I do not know. For the description of one incident, relating to Trinidadians on the *SS Coimbra* in September 1940, see CO859/40/12850/10c.
9. Colonial Office to the MWT, 12/4/44; minutes of a meeting between the Colonial Office, the Ministry of Labour and the MWT, 20/7/44, in CO937/6/3/22656.
10. In the words of the Cardiff Pool Registrar: *"West Indian seamen are not as a rule up to the normal standards of skill and discipline ... during the war they have adopted a decidedly cheeky attitude. In practice it is very difficult to place them ...* **there are plenty of white men available ..."** (emphasis mine). Quoted by the MWT in a letter to the Colonial Office, 2/9/44, ibid.
11. The US merchant marine, as the US navy, practised strict segregation, only employing Blacks in service categories. See Hugh Mulzac, *A Star to Steer By*, International Publishers, 1963.